# attitude Hairdos

# attitude

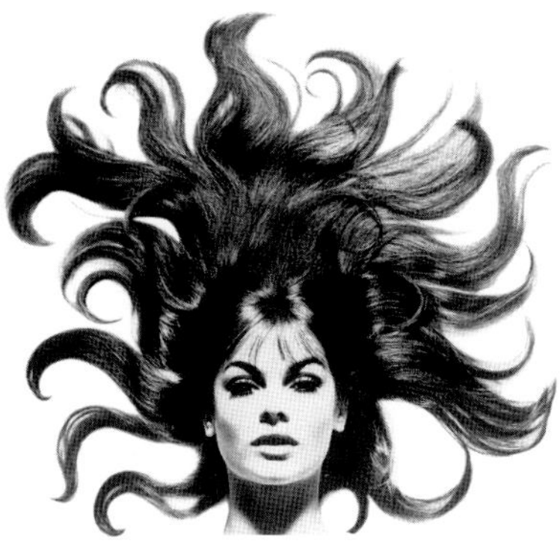

# Hairdos

MQP

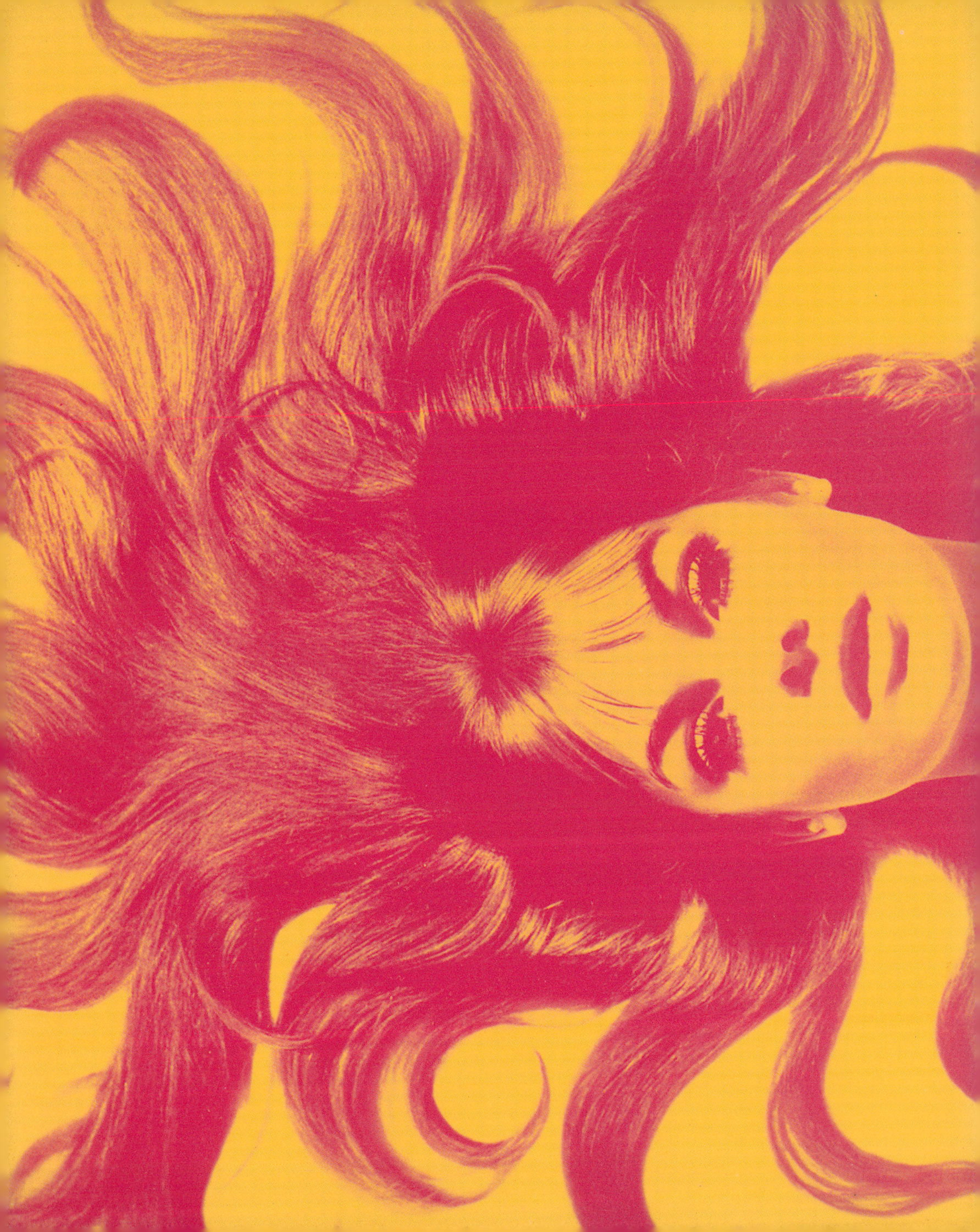

# Style V. Function

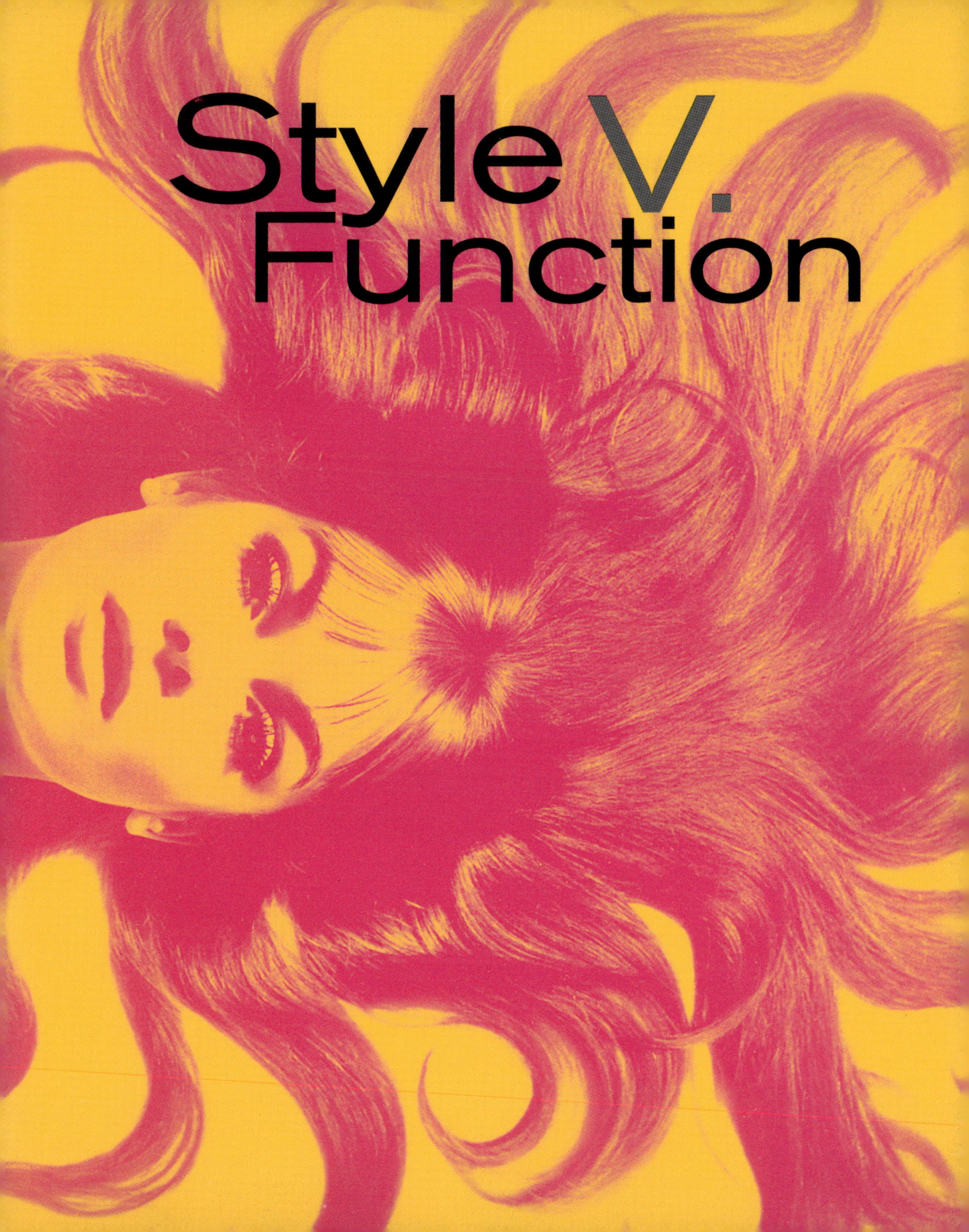

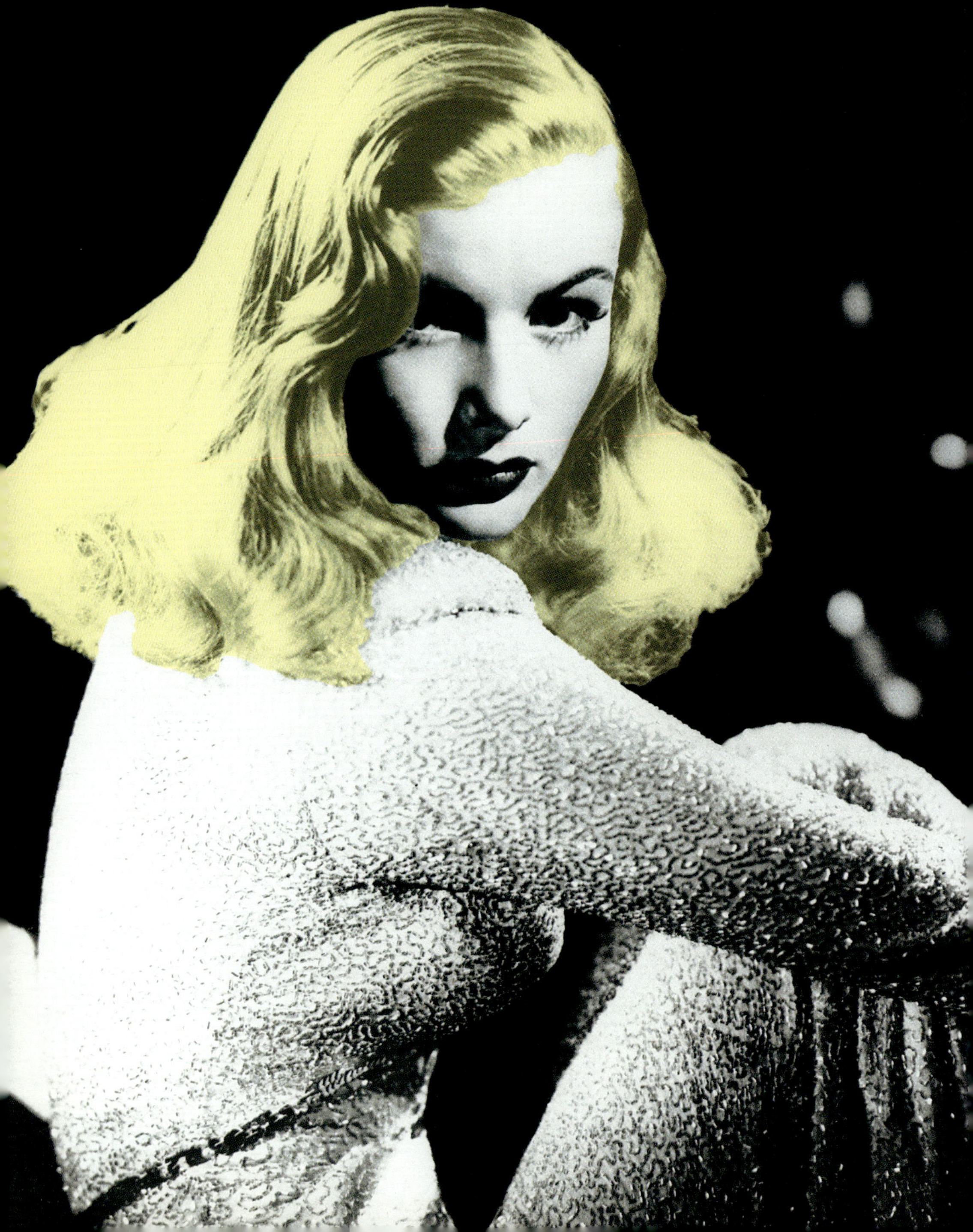

It was a blonde. A blonde to make a bishop kick a hole in a stained-glass window.

Raymond Chandler

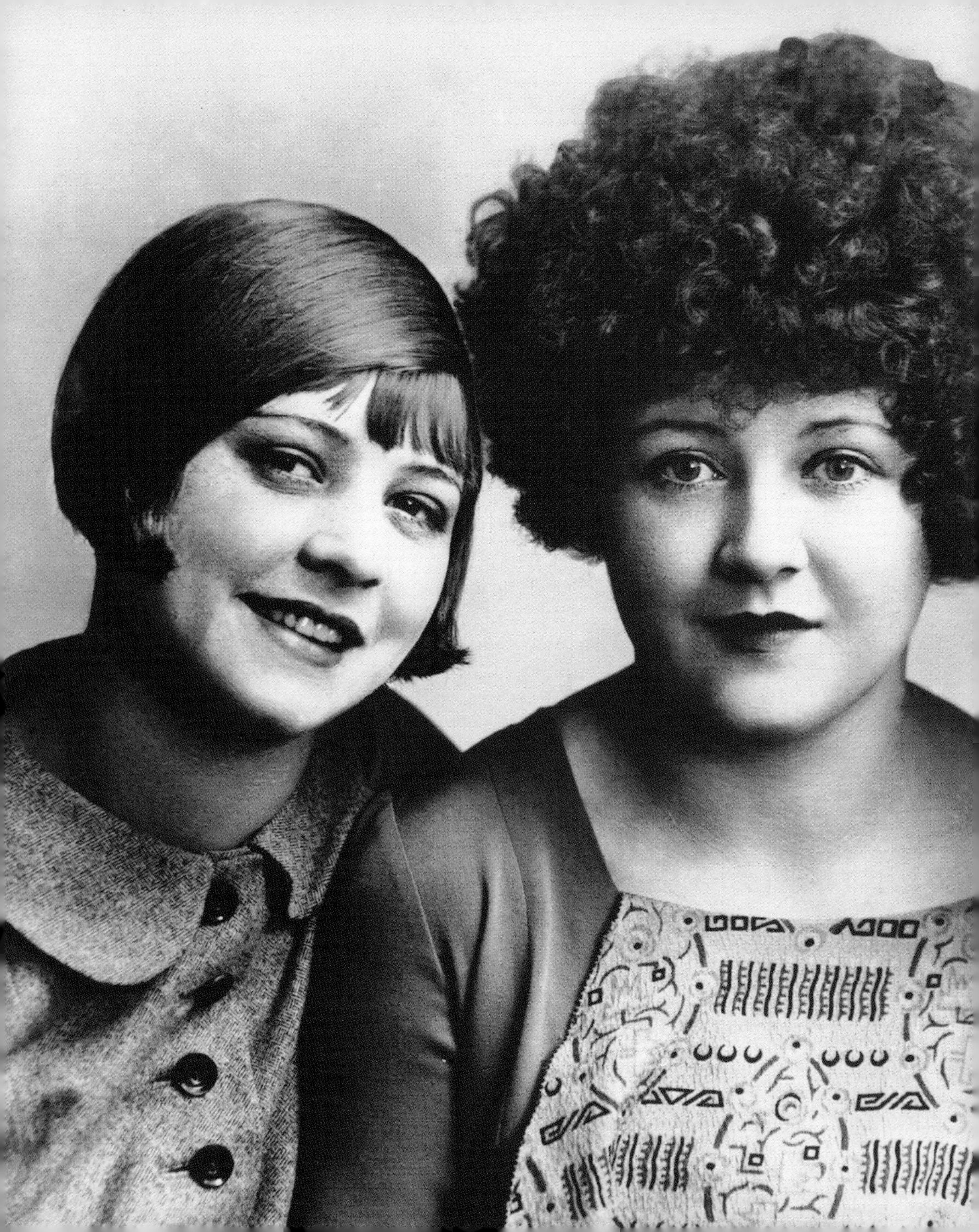

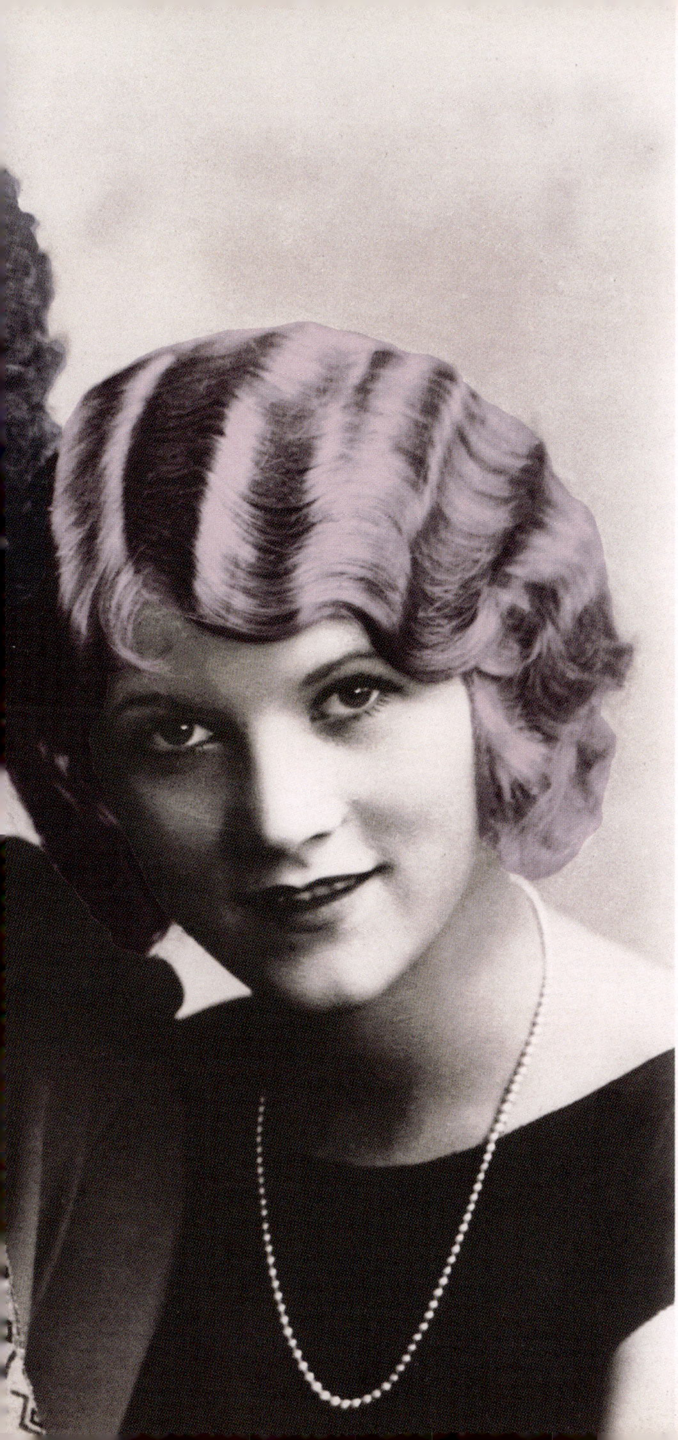

Violet will be
a good color
for hair at just
about the same
time that brunette
becomes a good
color for flowers.

FRAN LEBOWITZ

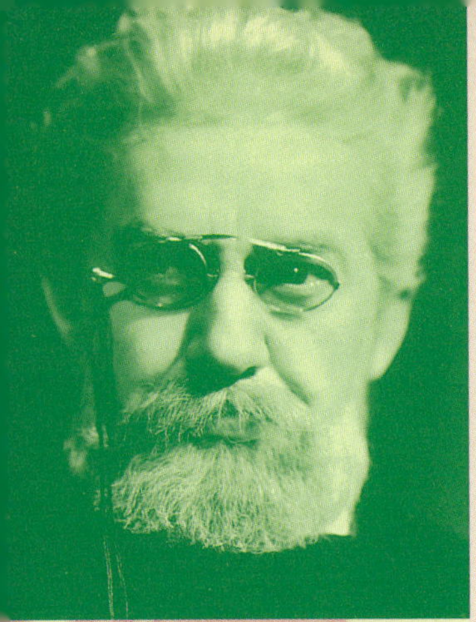

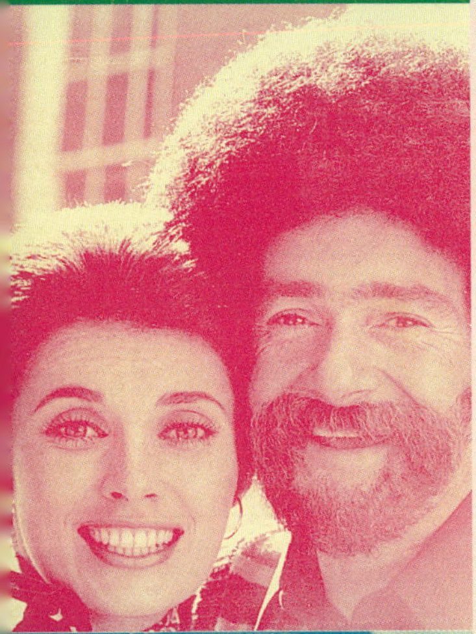

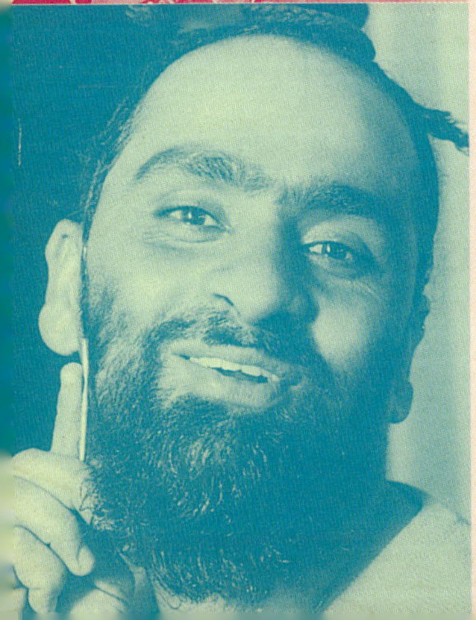

It always seemed to me that men wore their beards, like they wear their neckties, for show.

D.H. Lawrence

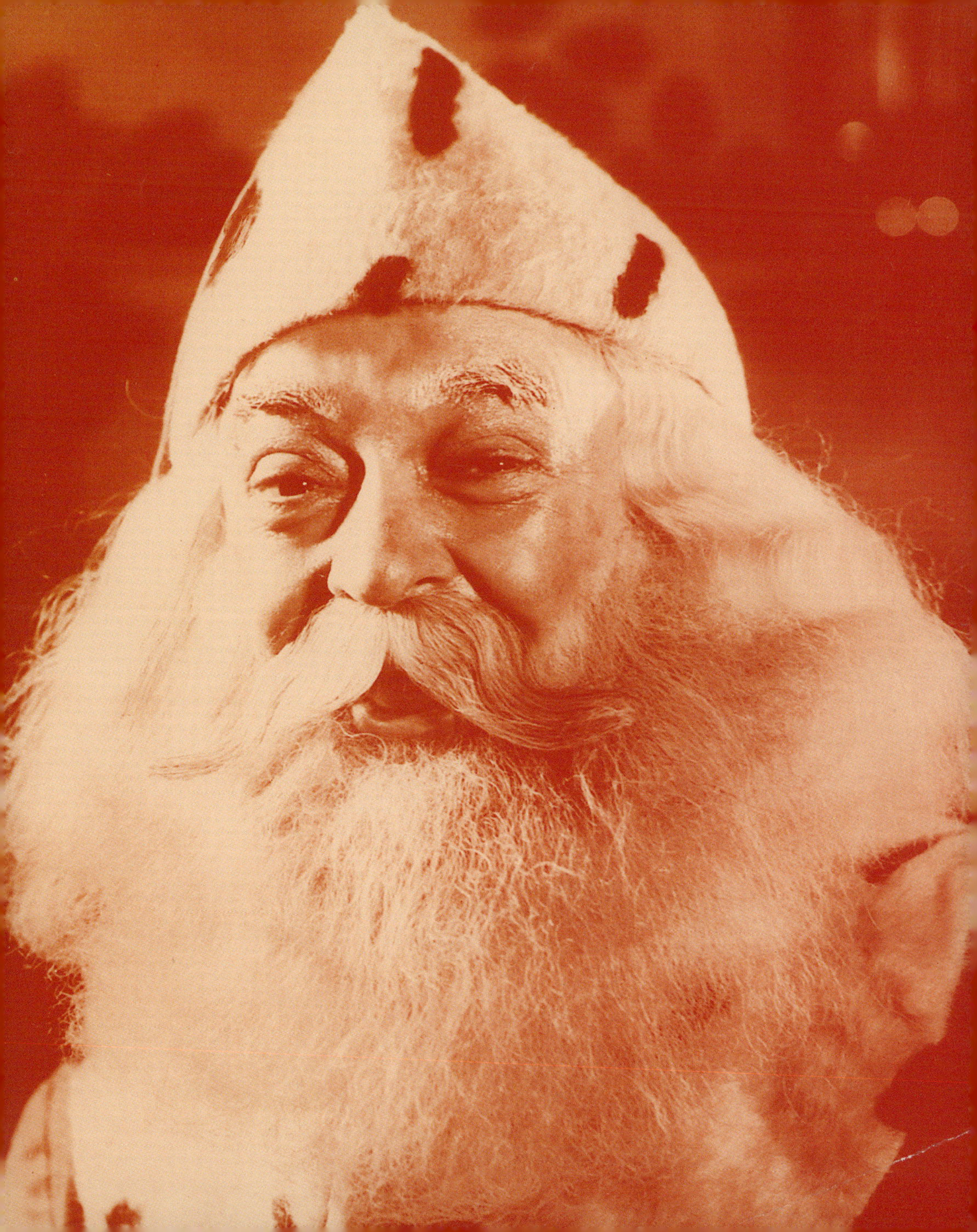

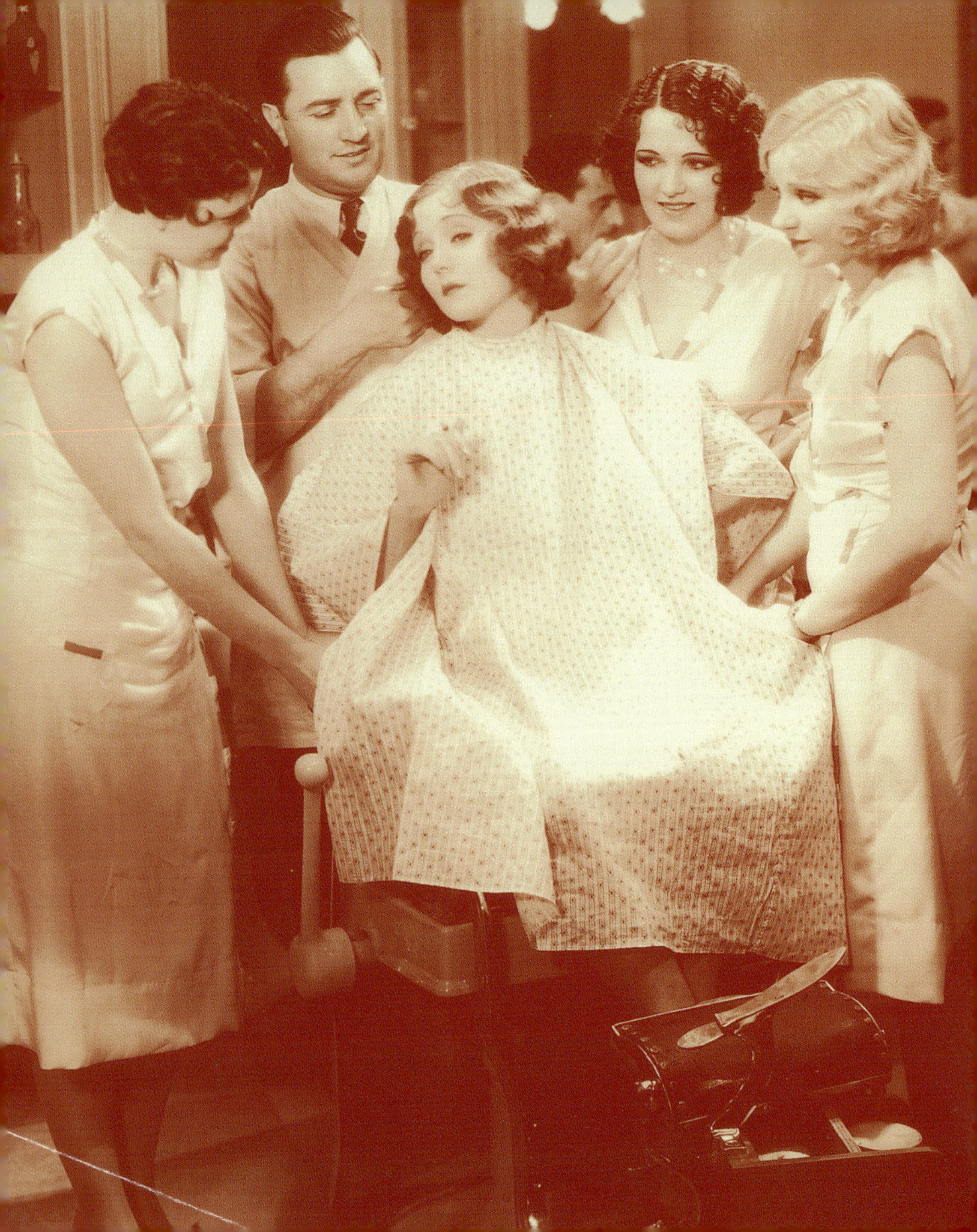

If truth is beauty,
how come no one
has their hair
done in the library?

LILY TOMLIN

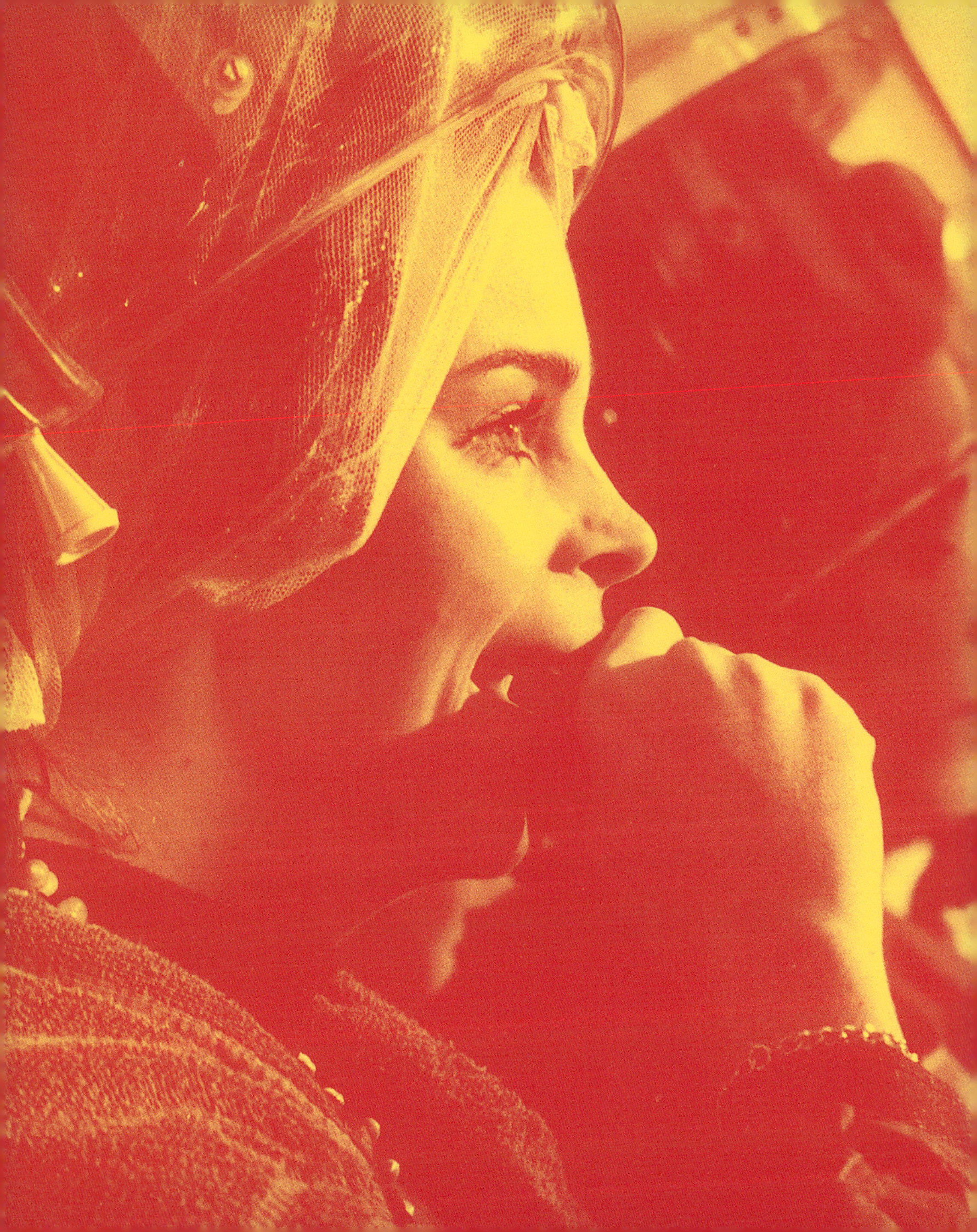

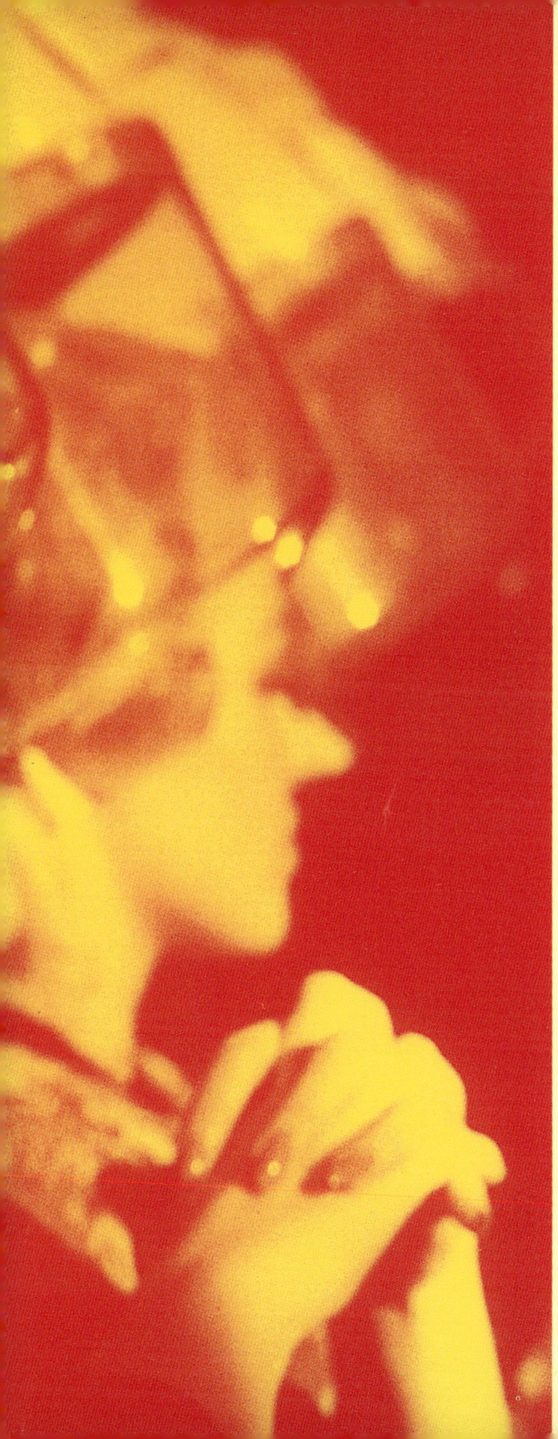

**To Crystal, hair was the most important thing on earth. She would never get married because you couldn't wear curlers in bed.**

**Edna O'Brien**

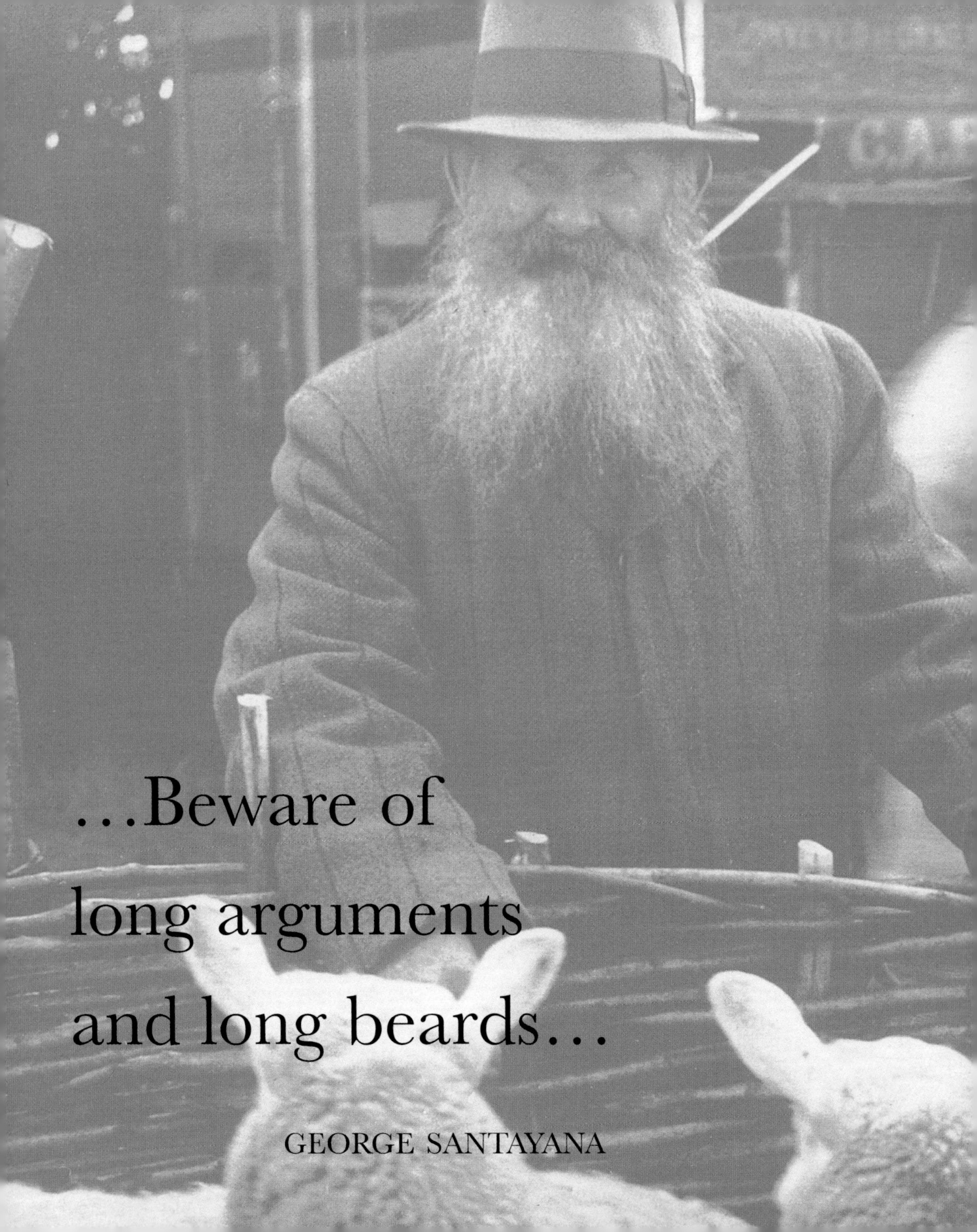

...Beware of long arguments and long beards...

GEORGE SANTAYANA

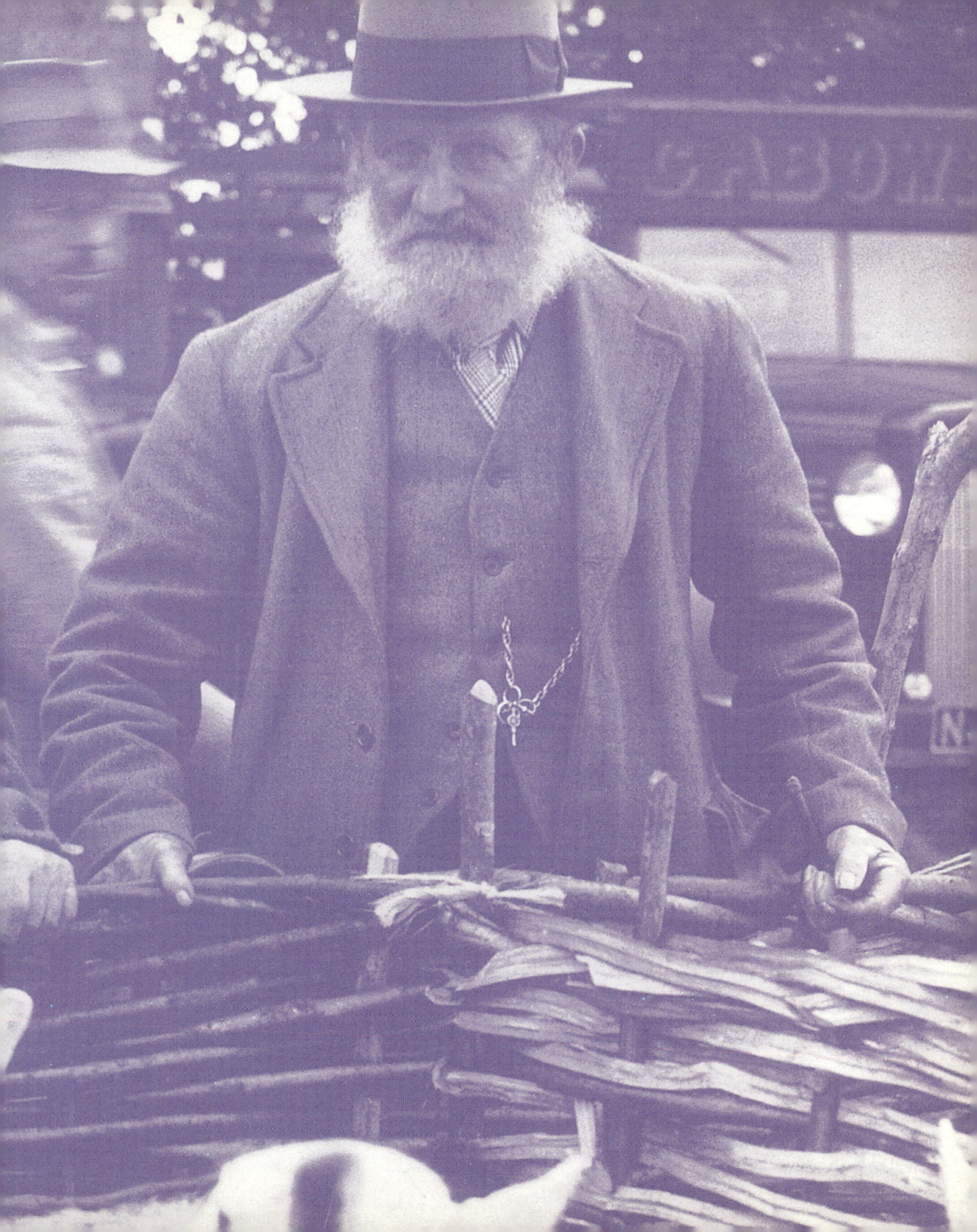

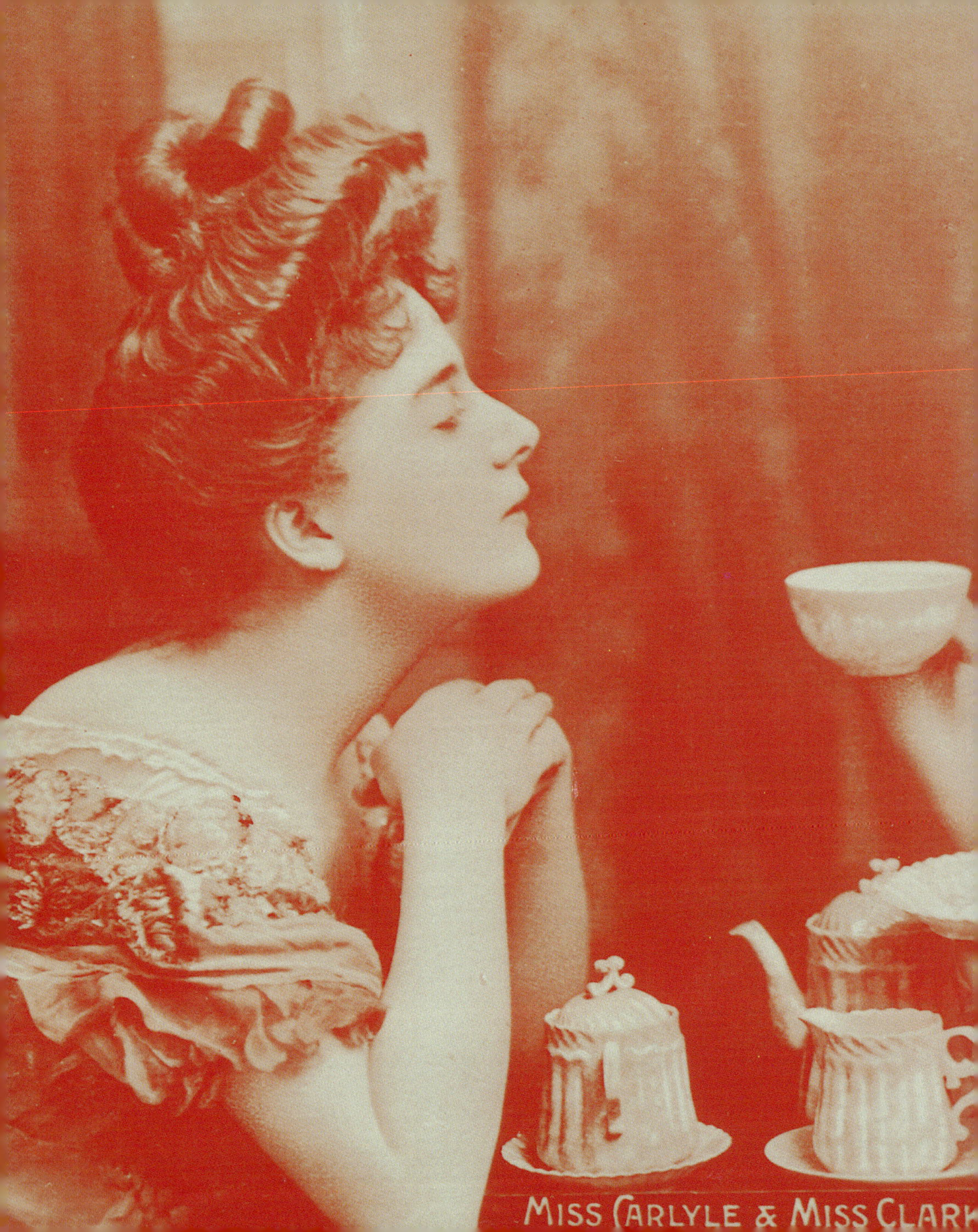
MISS CARLYLE & MISS CLARK

# HAIR RAISING

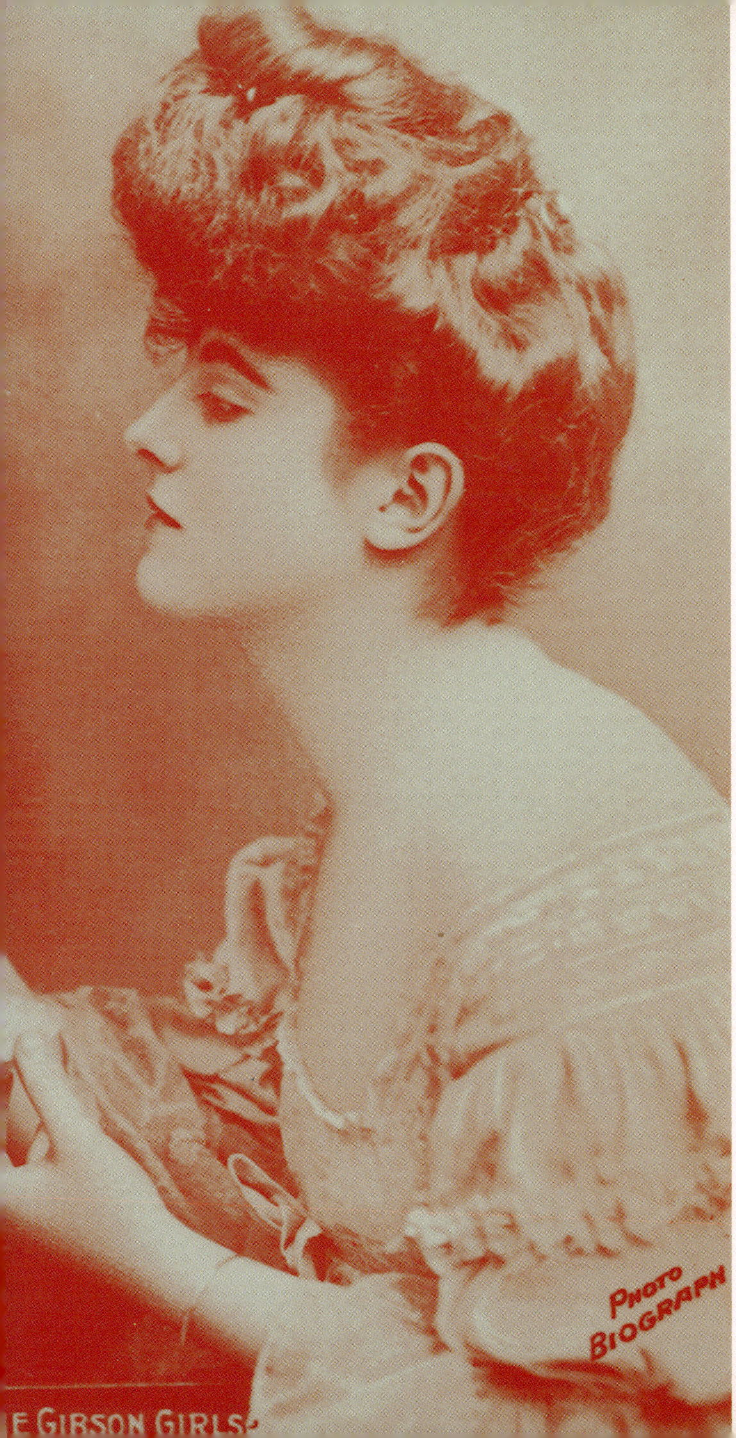

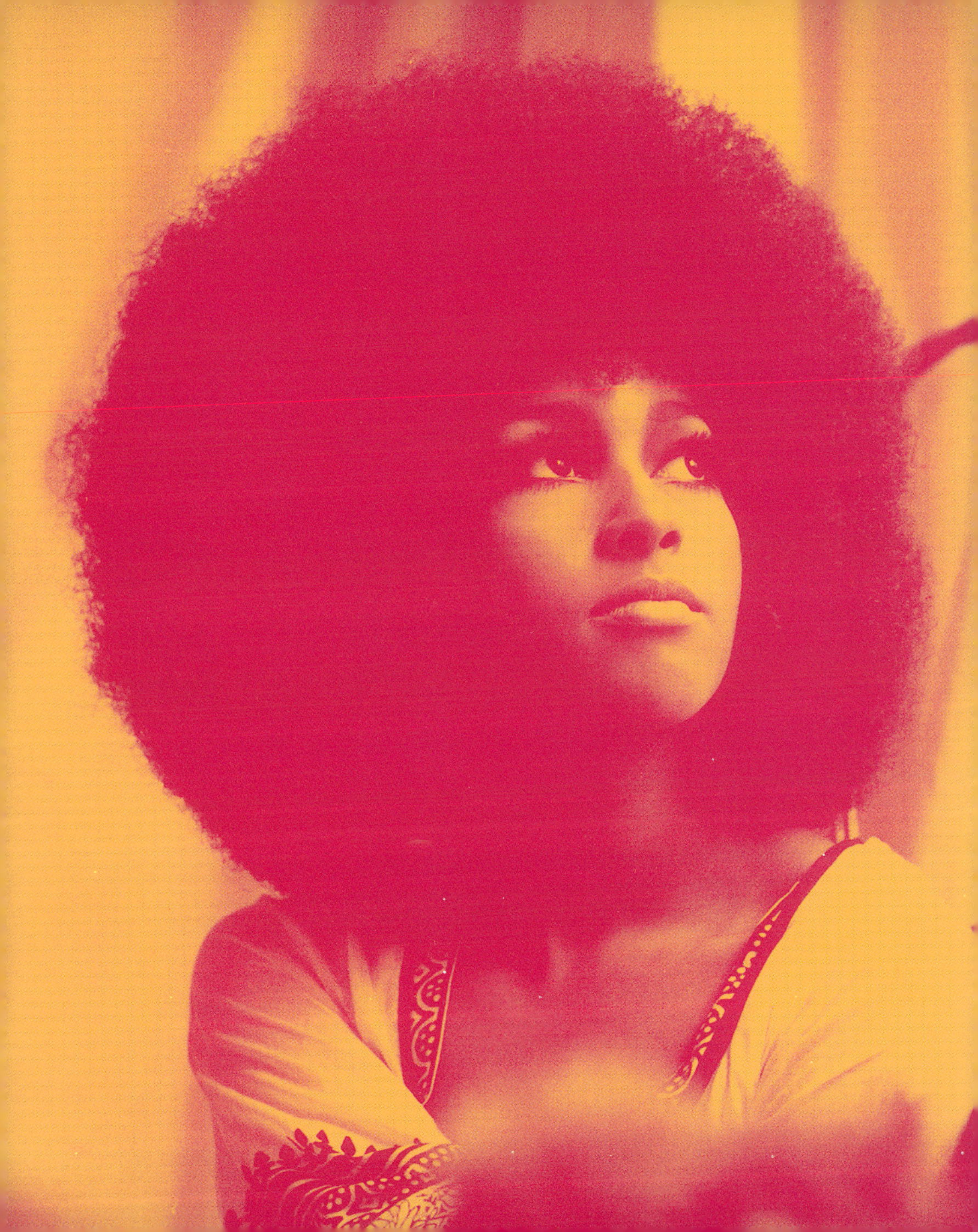

**Long**, *beautiful*,
gleaming,
**steaming**,
flaxen, *waxen...*
**'I adore hair!'**

**from the musical *HAIR***

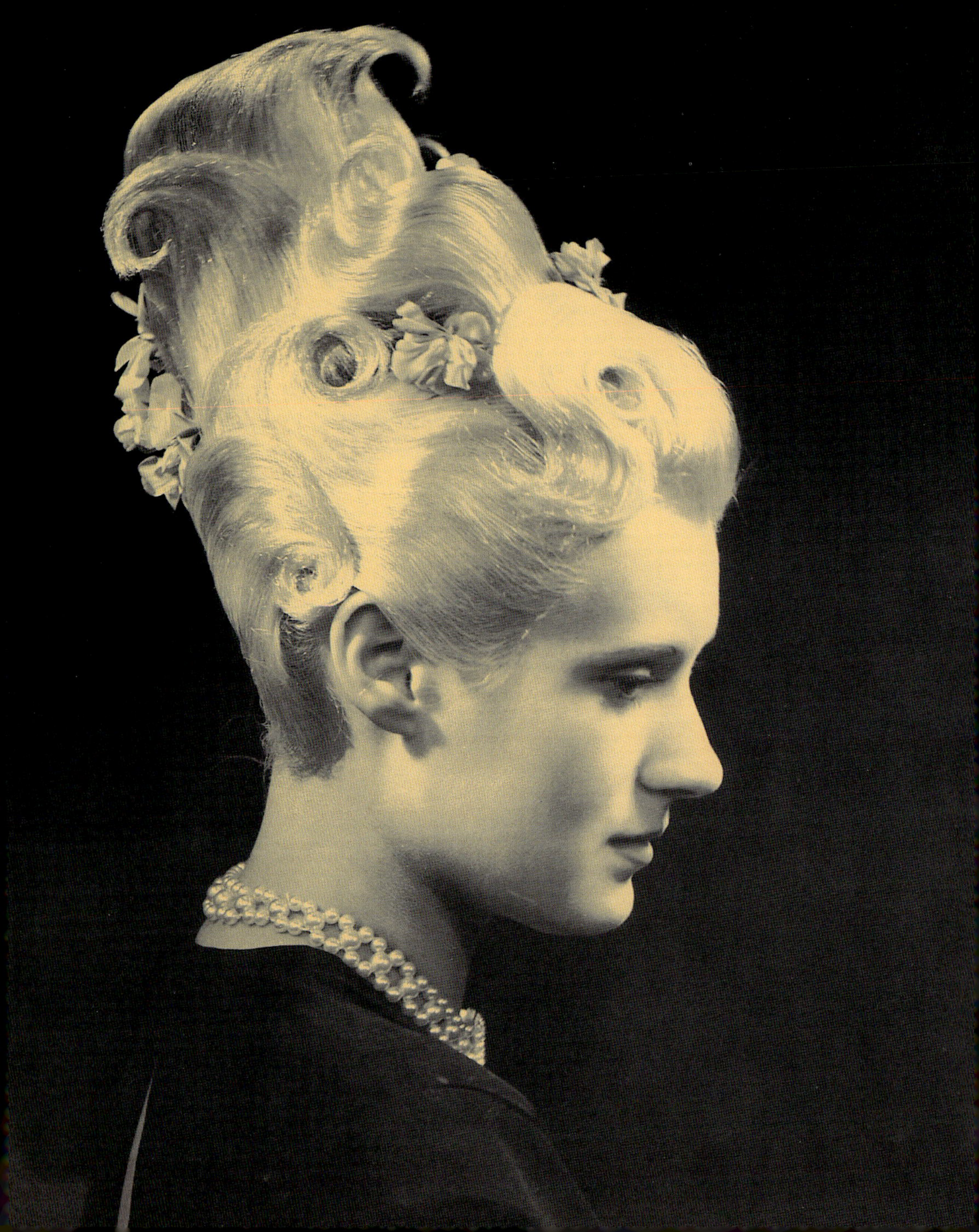

Only God, my dear,
Could love you for
yourself alone
And not your
yellow hair.

W.B. Yeats

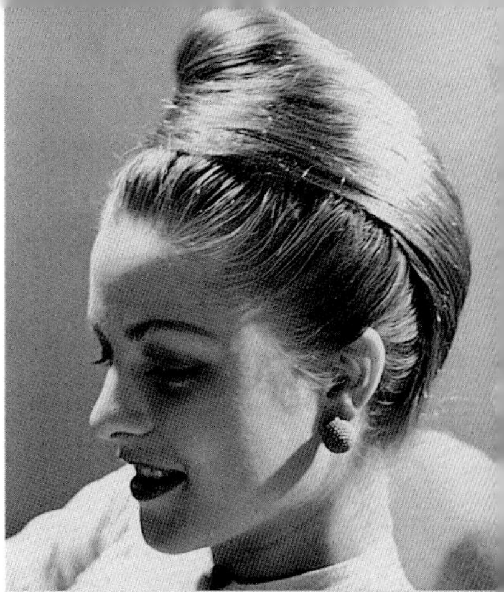

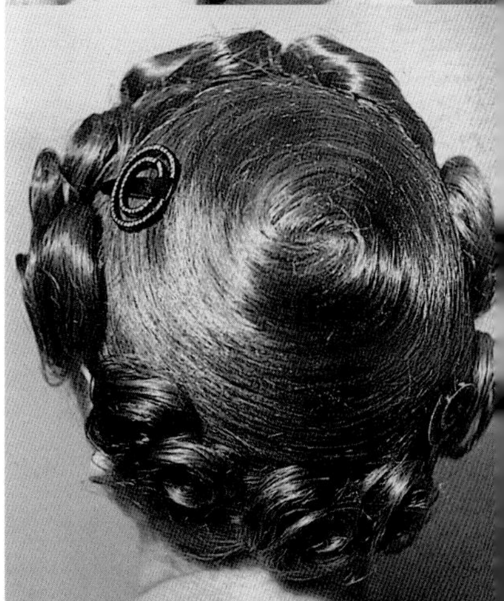

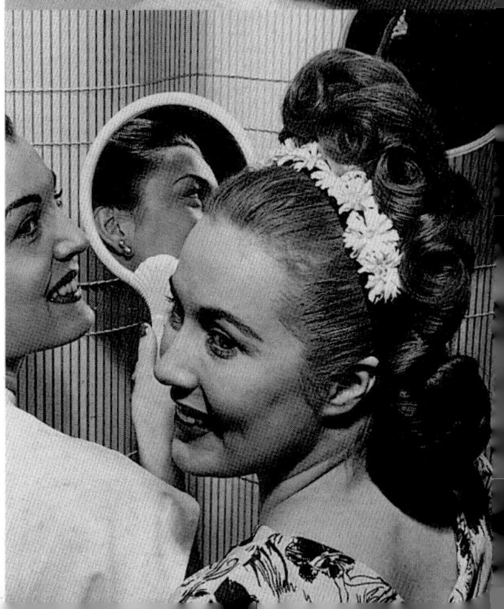

**There is nothing more contemptible than a bald man who pretends to have hair.**

**Martial, Epigrams**

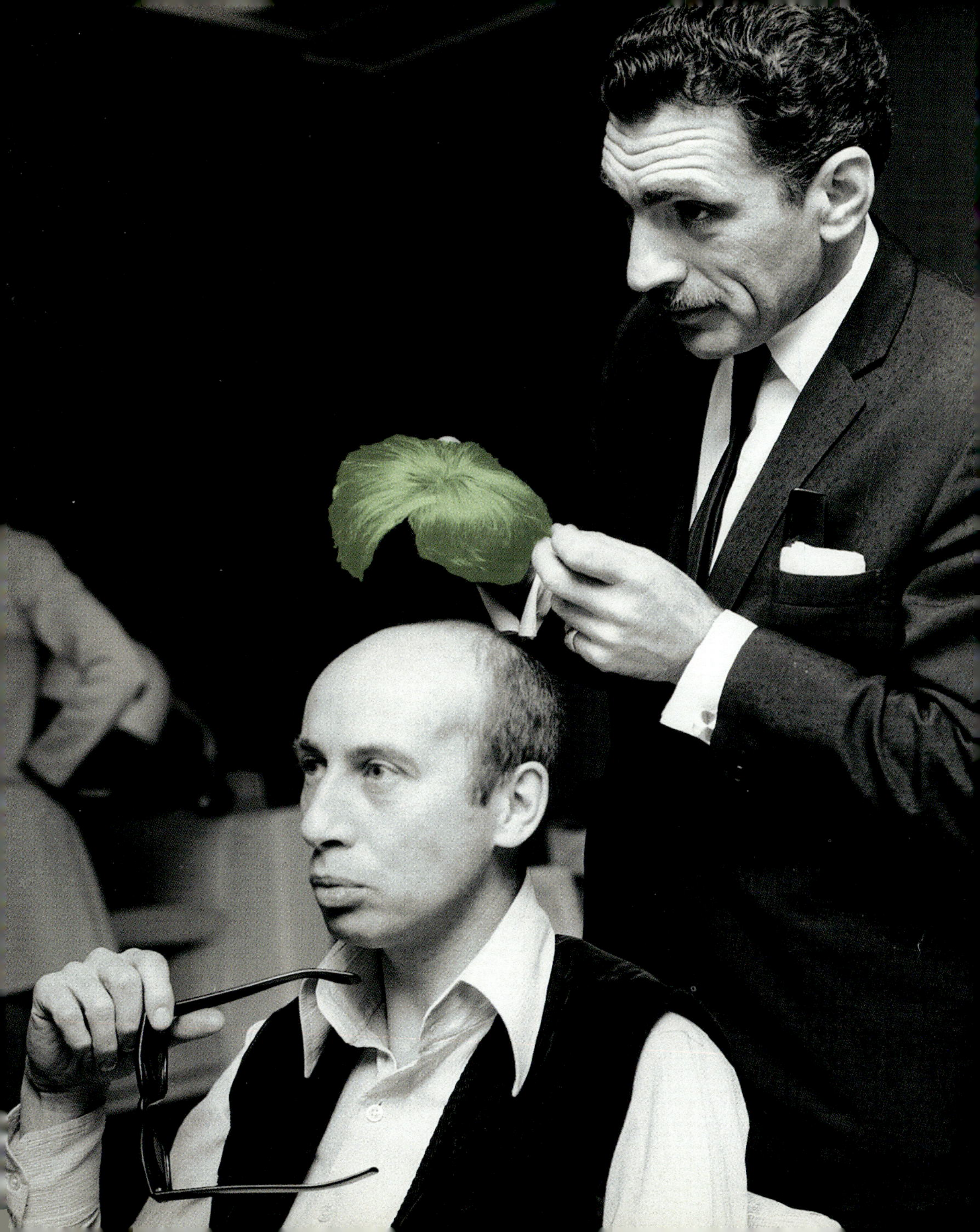

And, while she feels
the heavens lie
bare,
She only talks
about her hair.

FRANCIS THOMPSON,
*THE WAY OF A MAID*

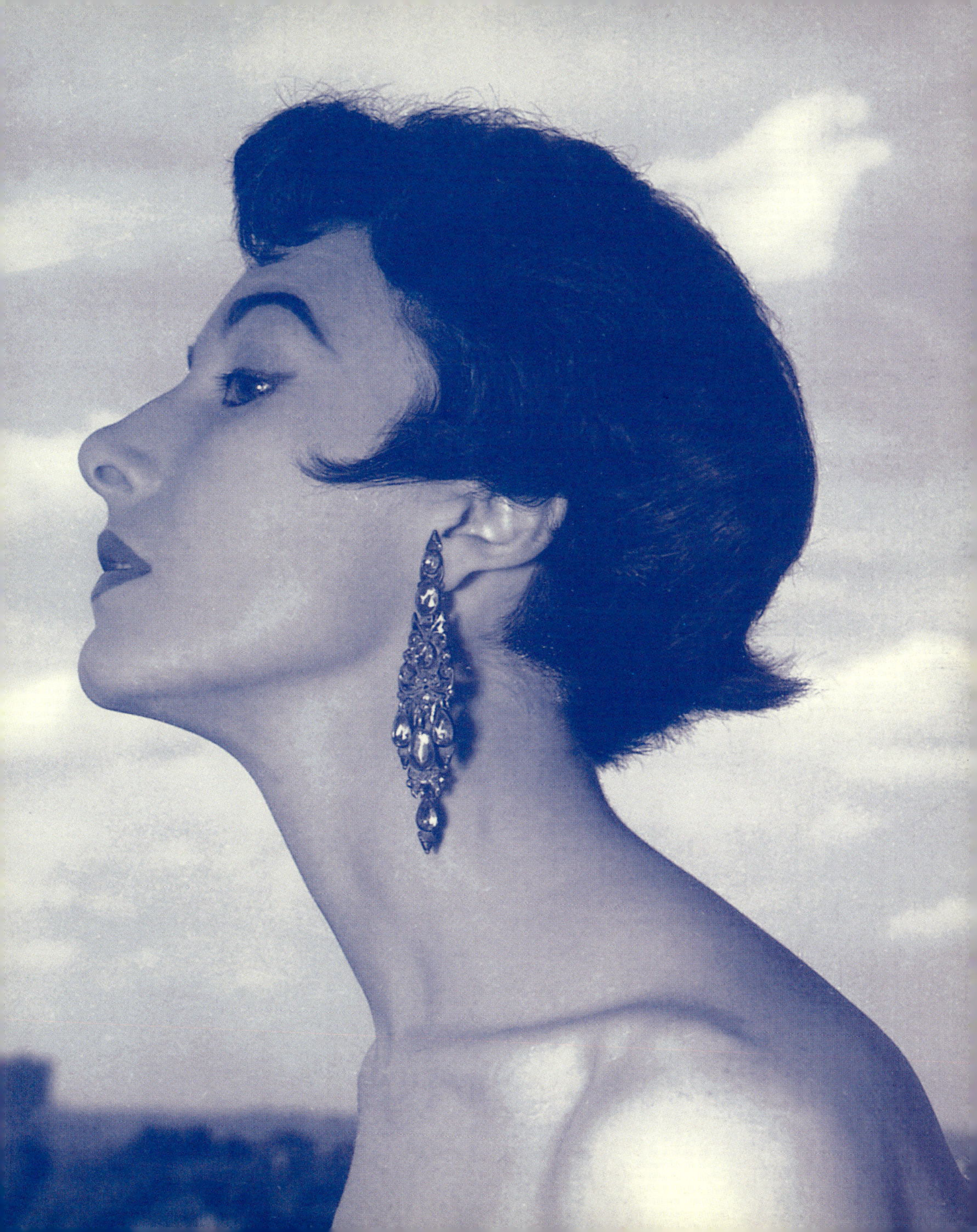

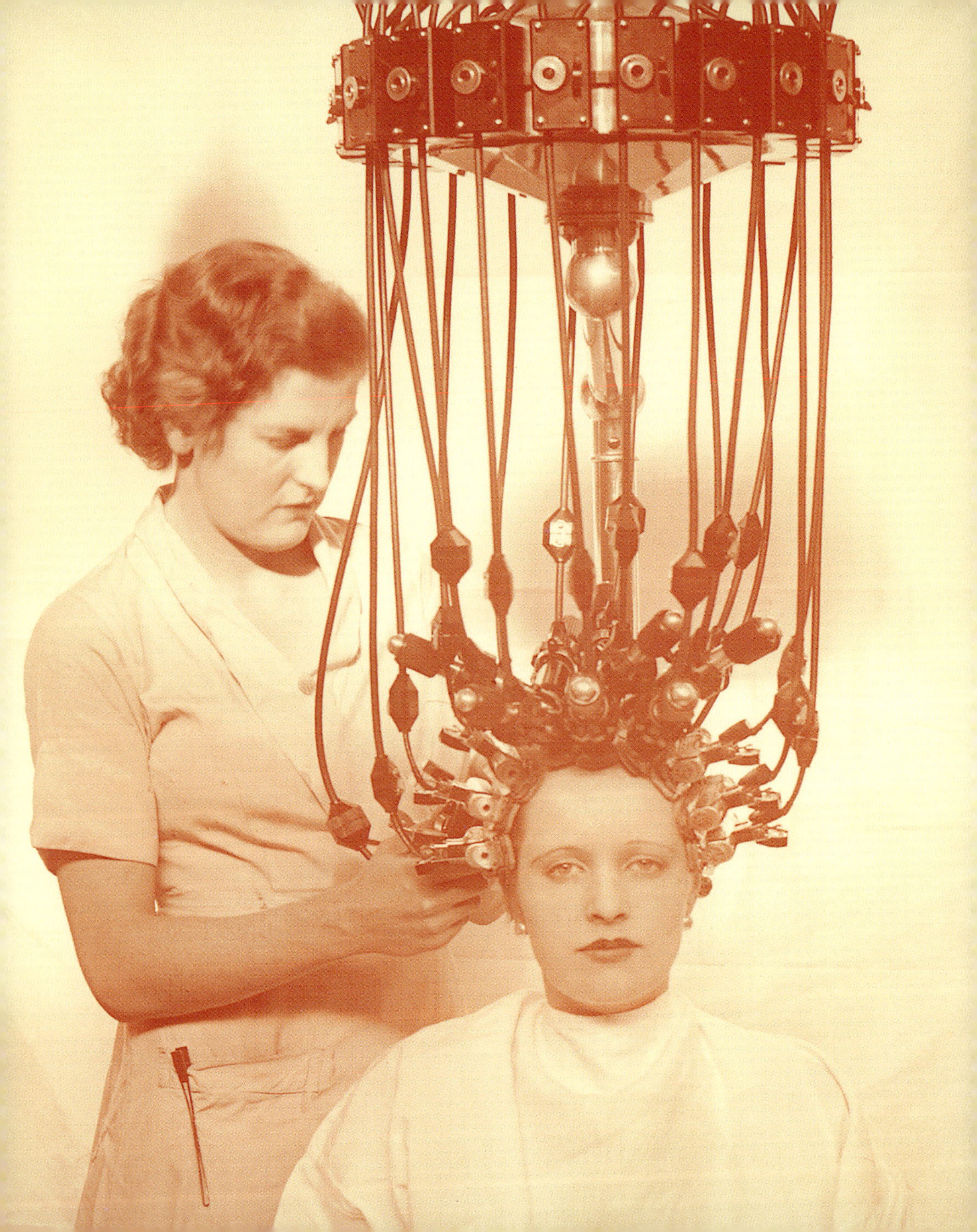

Everything is funny as long as it is happening to somebody else.

Will Rogers

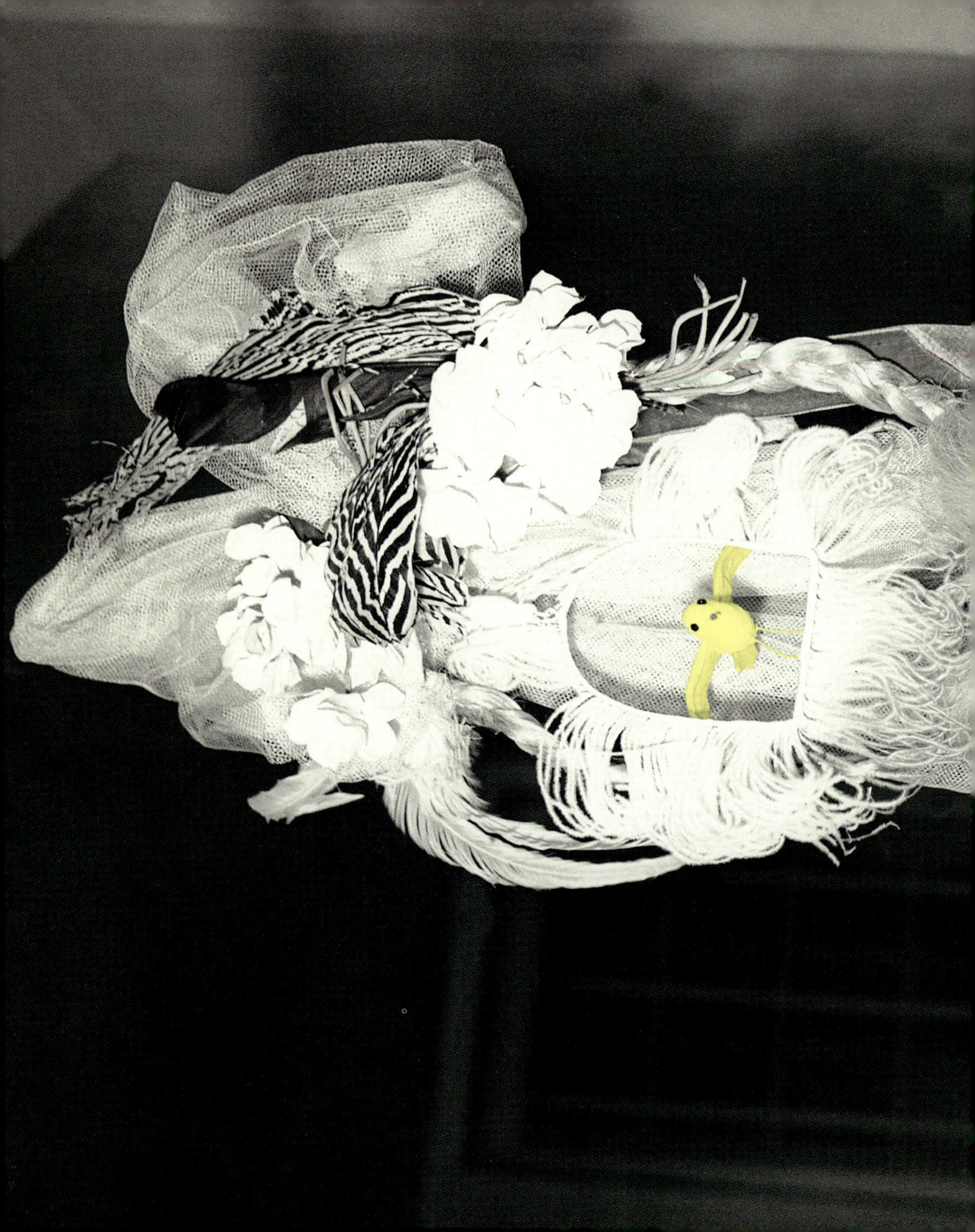

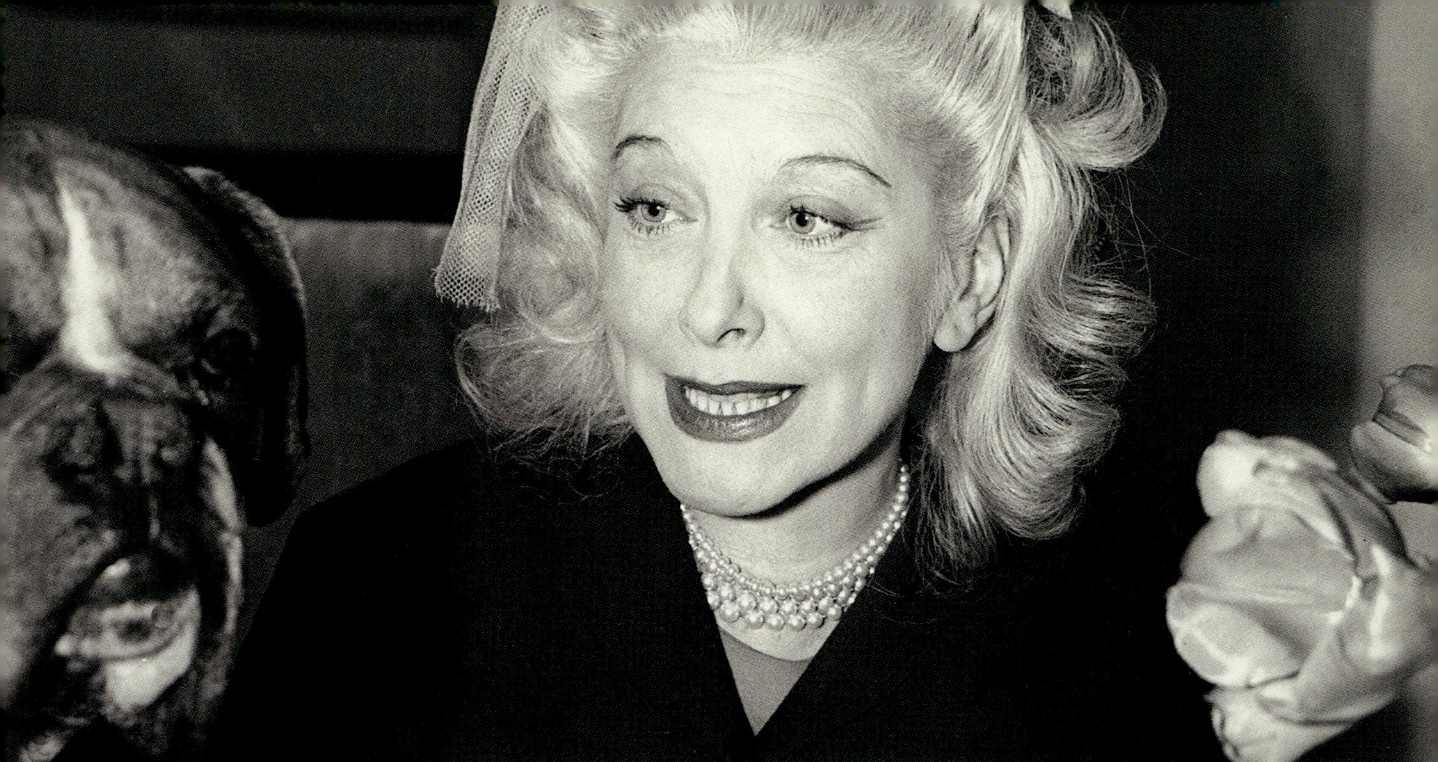

# HAIRBRAINED

# WORK/STRE

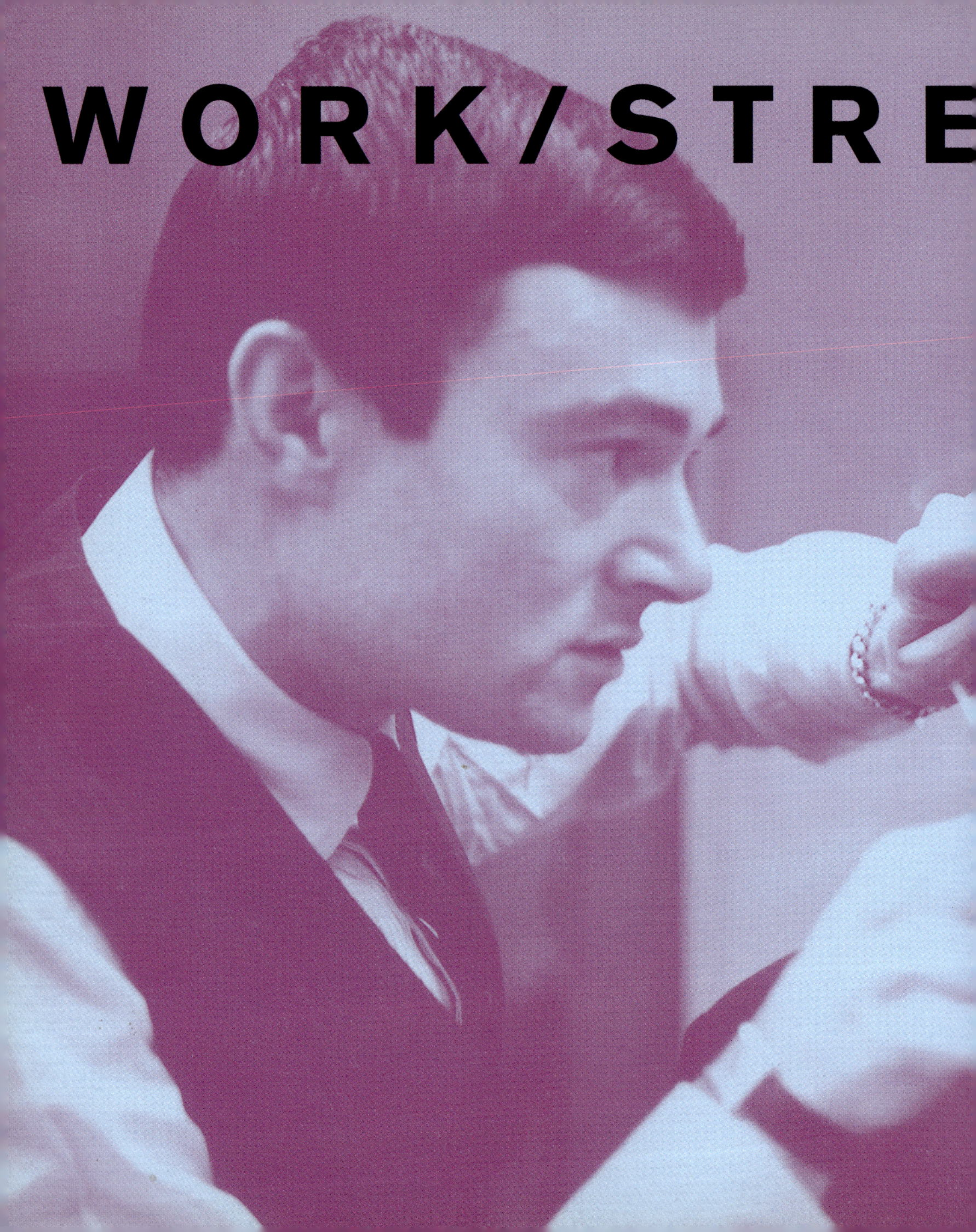

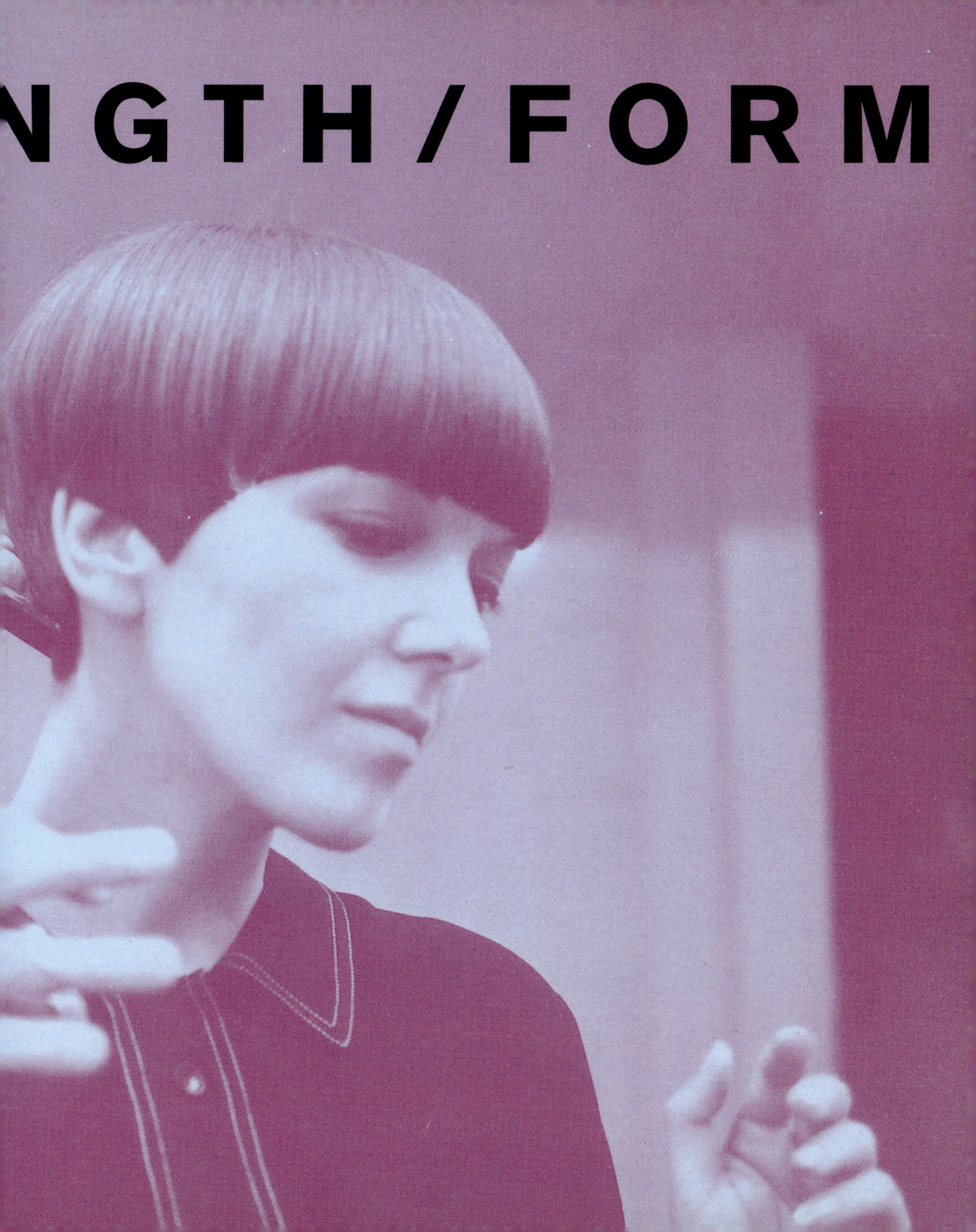
NGTH / FORM

Beauty draws
us with a
single hair.

ALEXANDER POPE

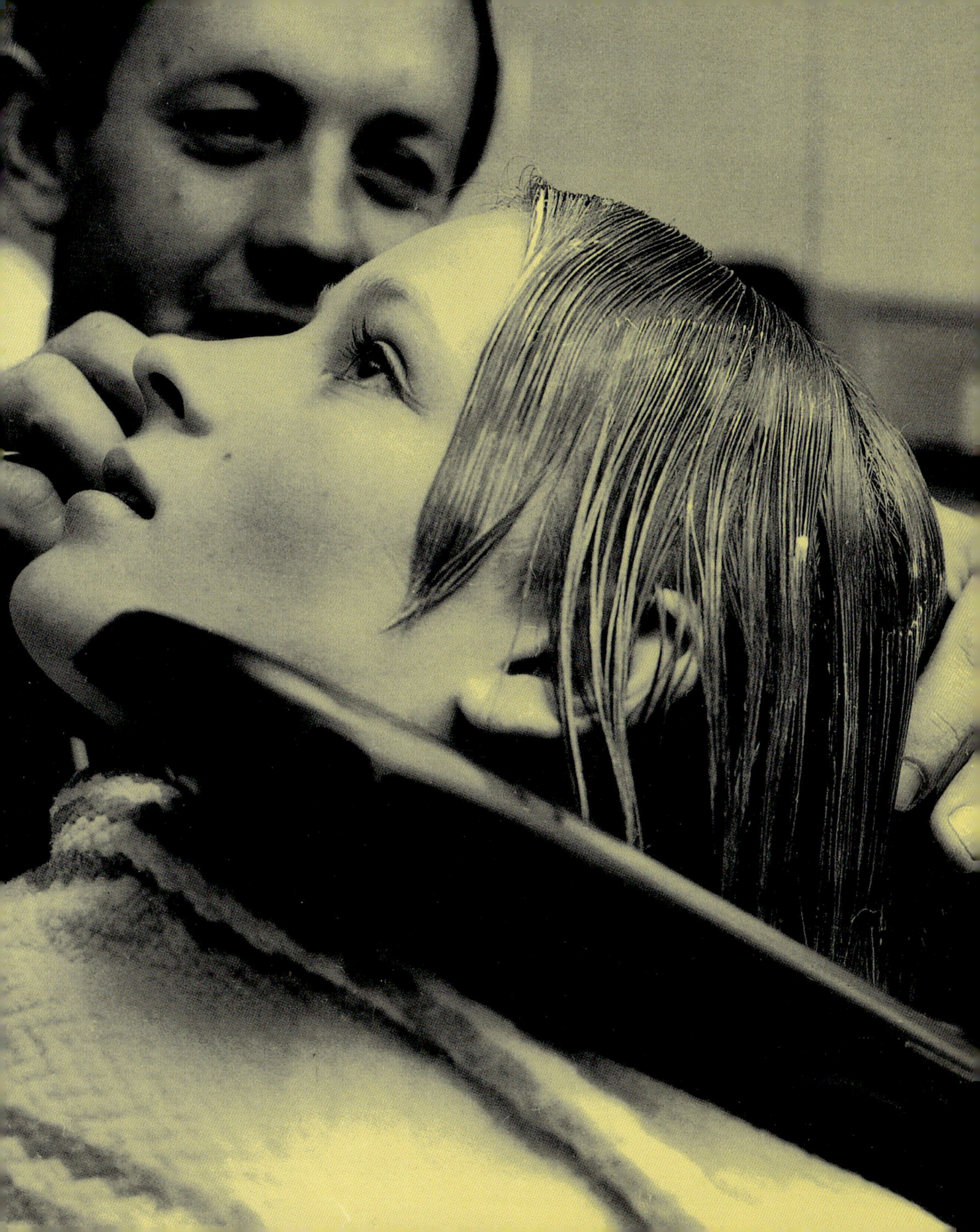

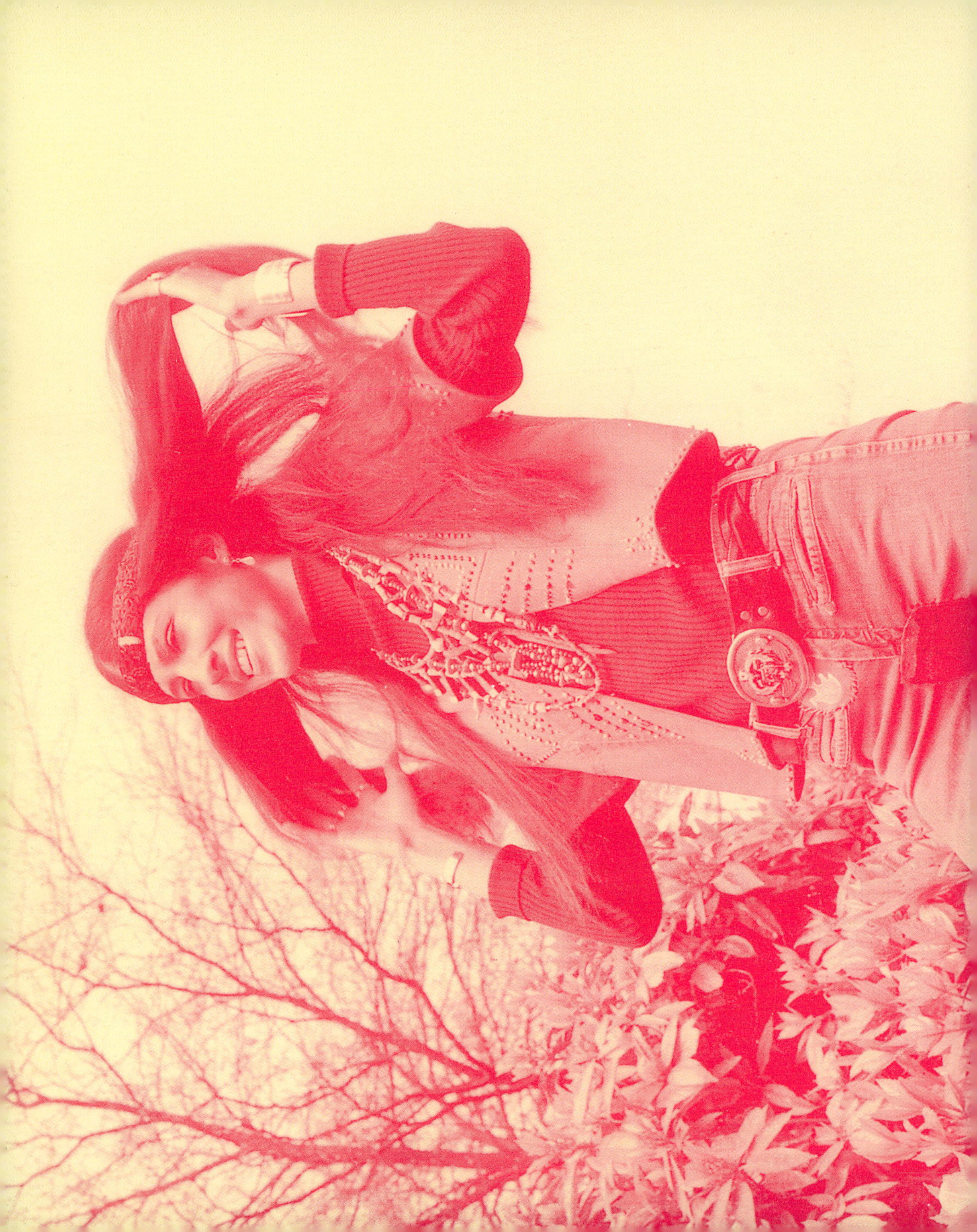

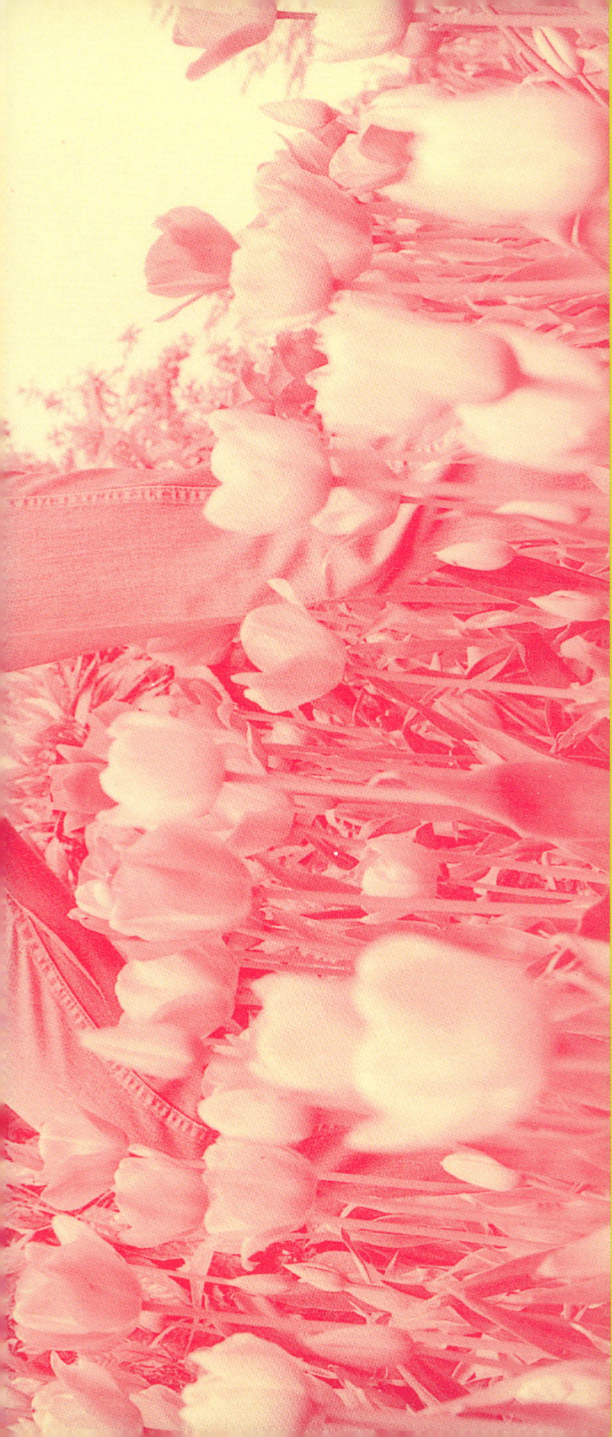

And forget not
that the earth
delights to feel
your bare feet
and the winds
long to play with
your hair.

Kahlil Gibran

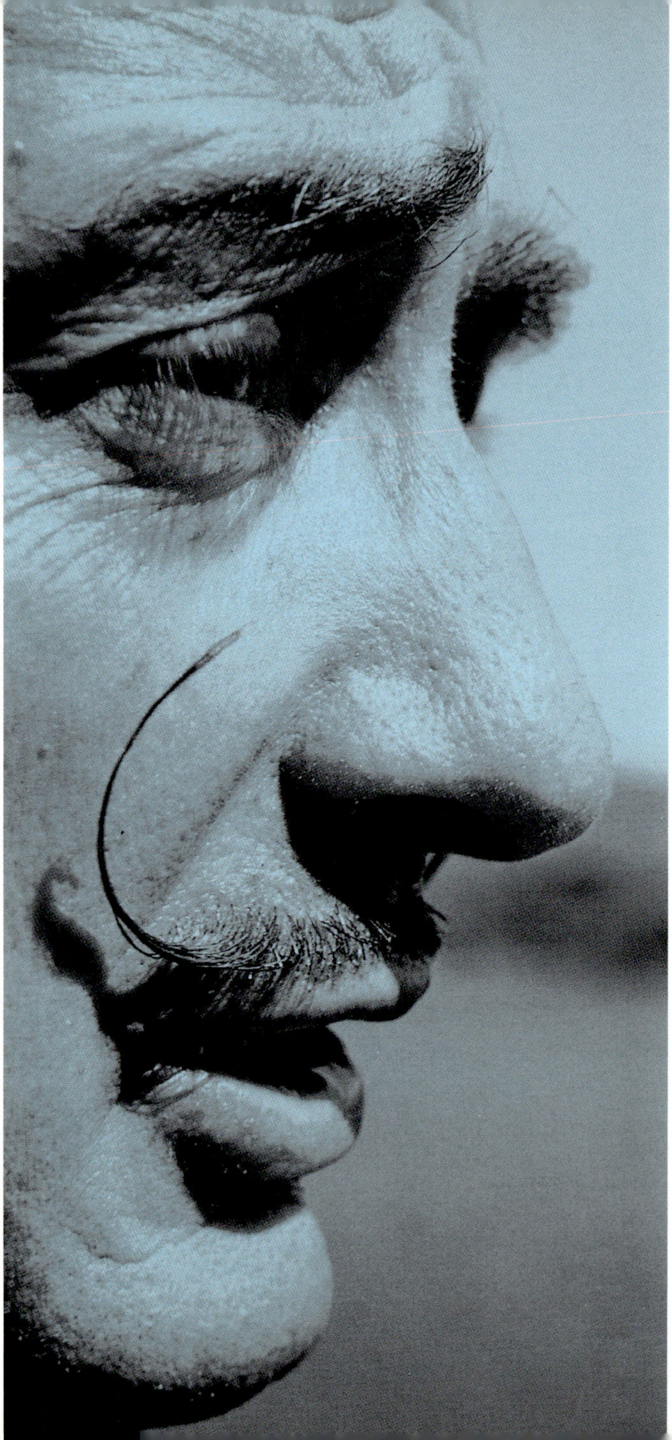

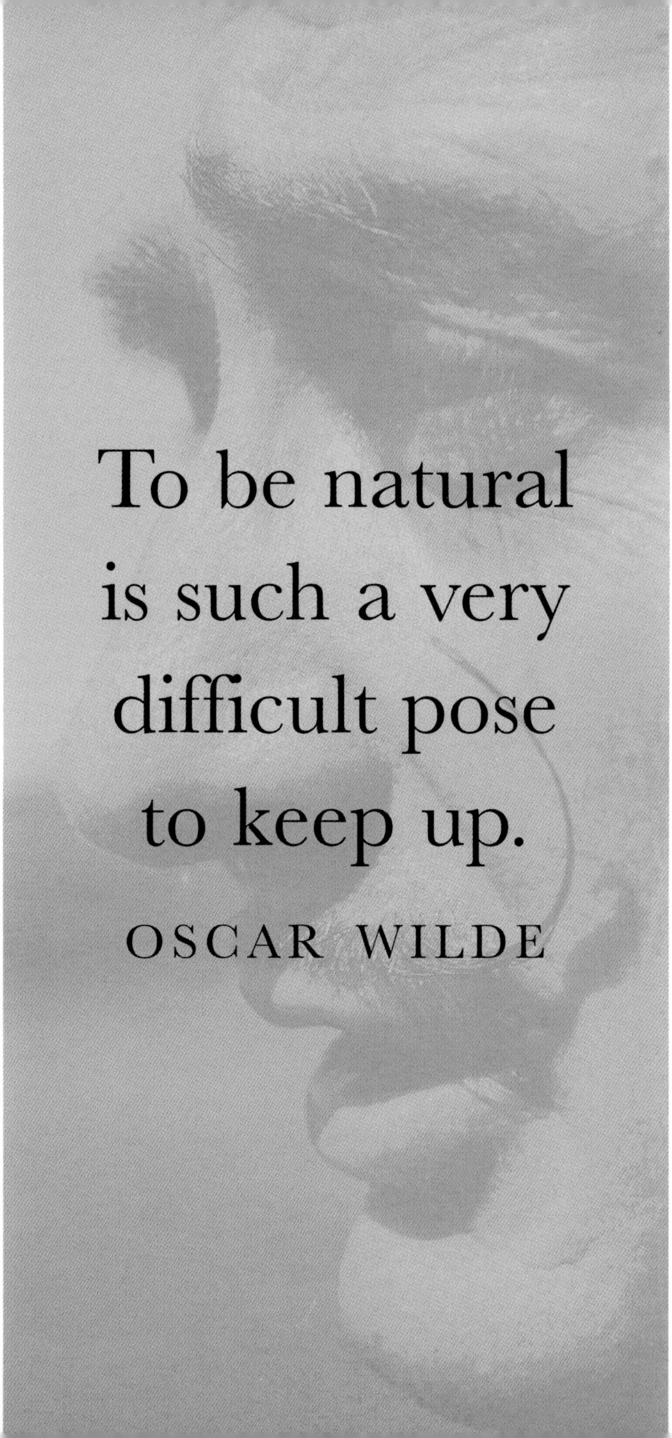

To be natural
is such a very
difficult pose
to keep up.

OSCAR WILDE

I see the Beatles have arrived from England. They were forty pounds overweight, and that was just their hair.

Bob Hope



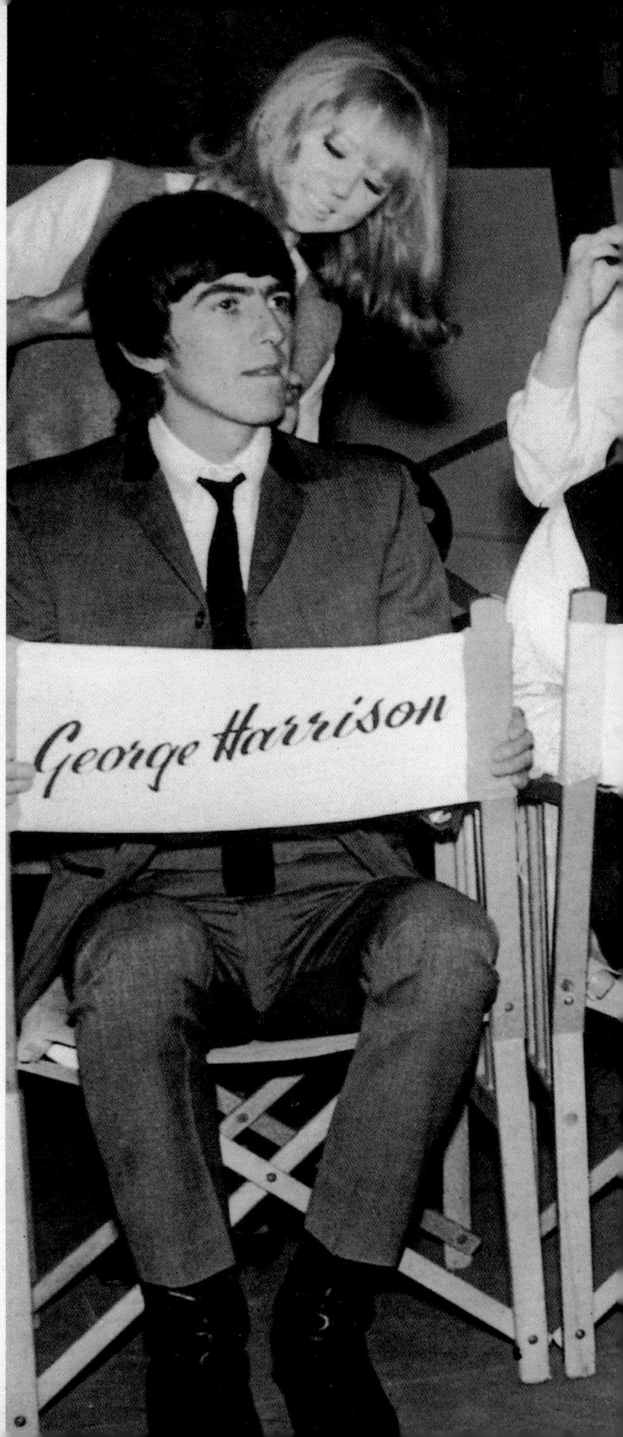

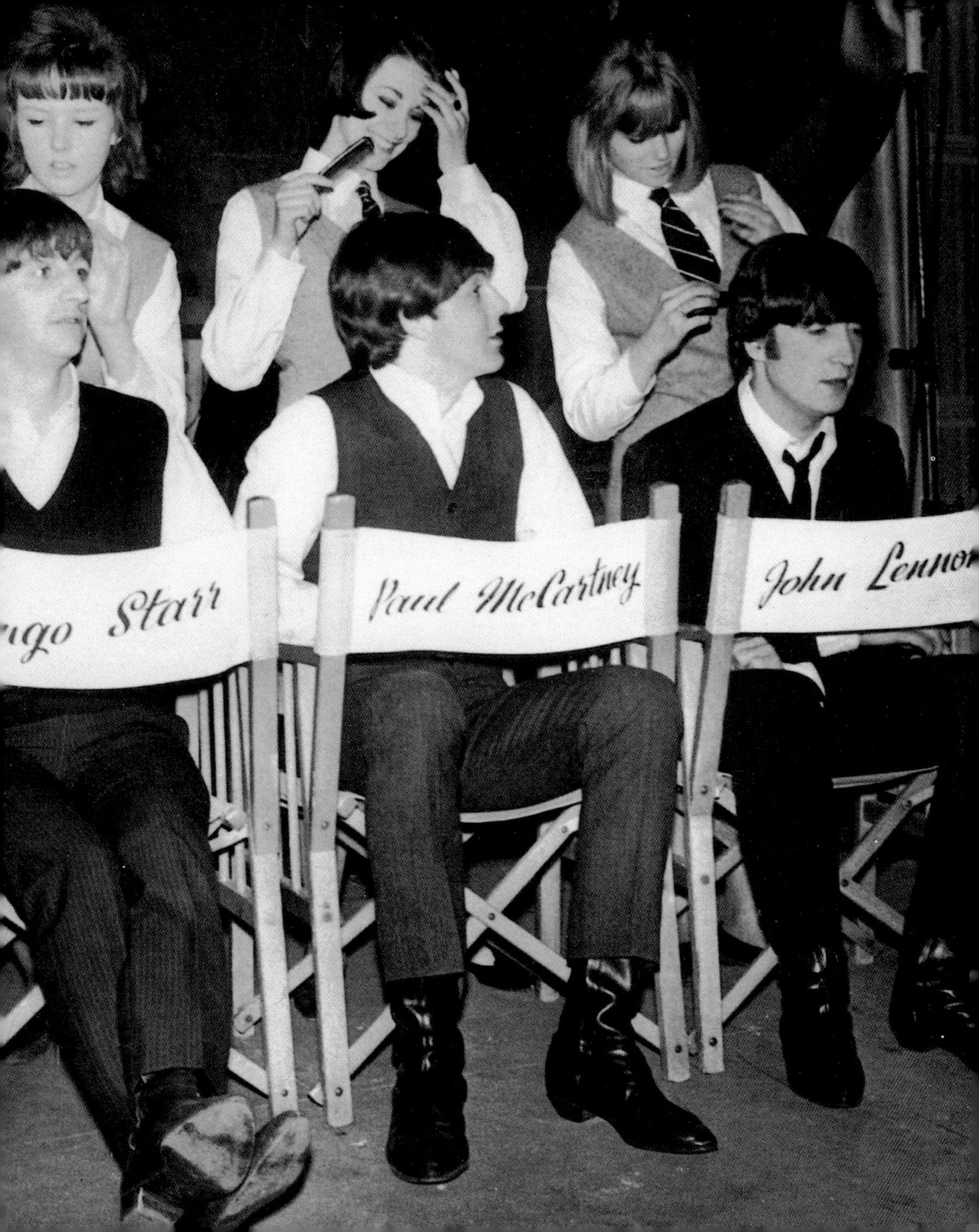
ngo Starr
Paul McCartney
John Lennon

**Between the cradle
and the grave
Lies a haircut and a
shave.**

**Samuel Hoffenstein**

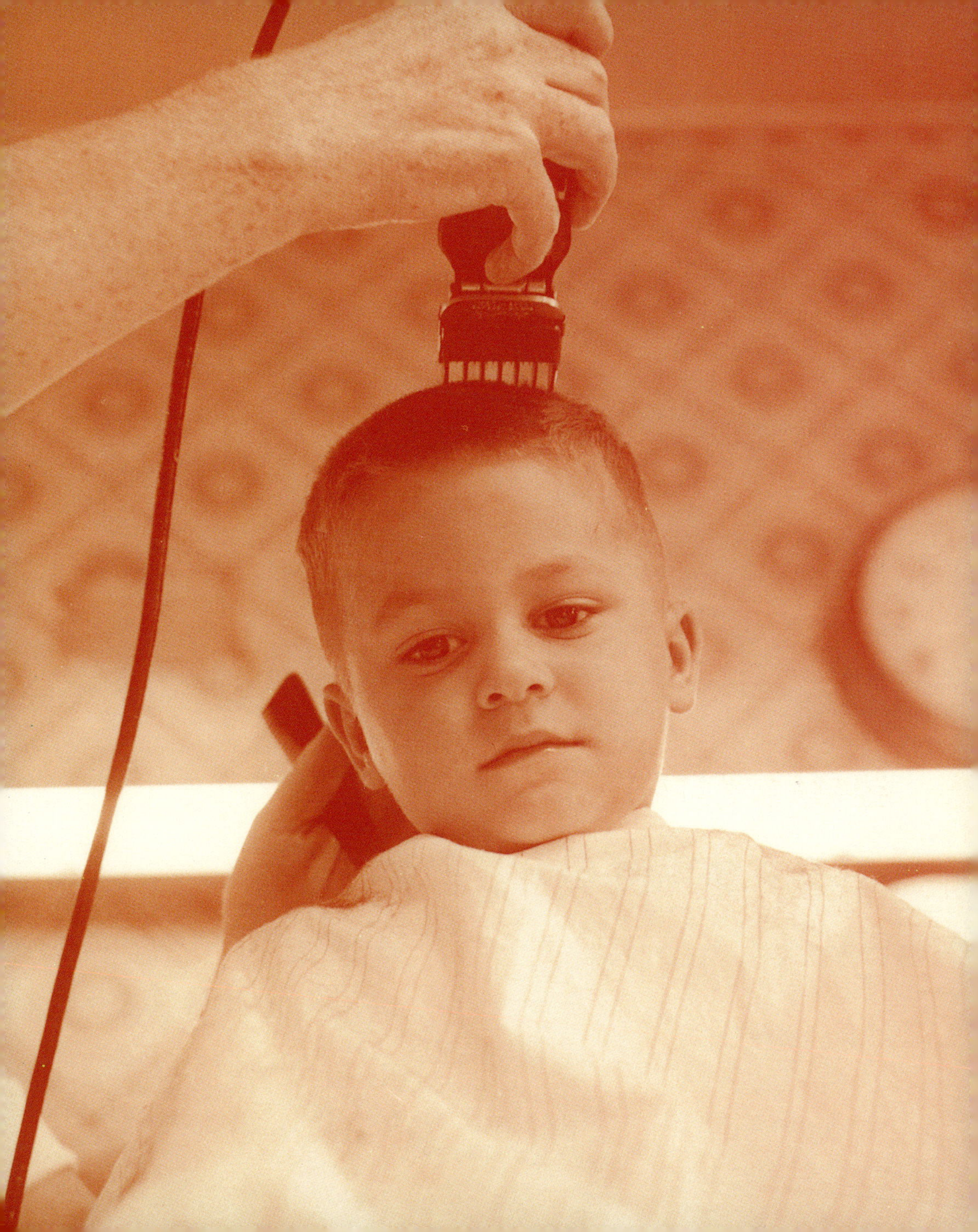

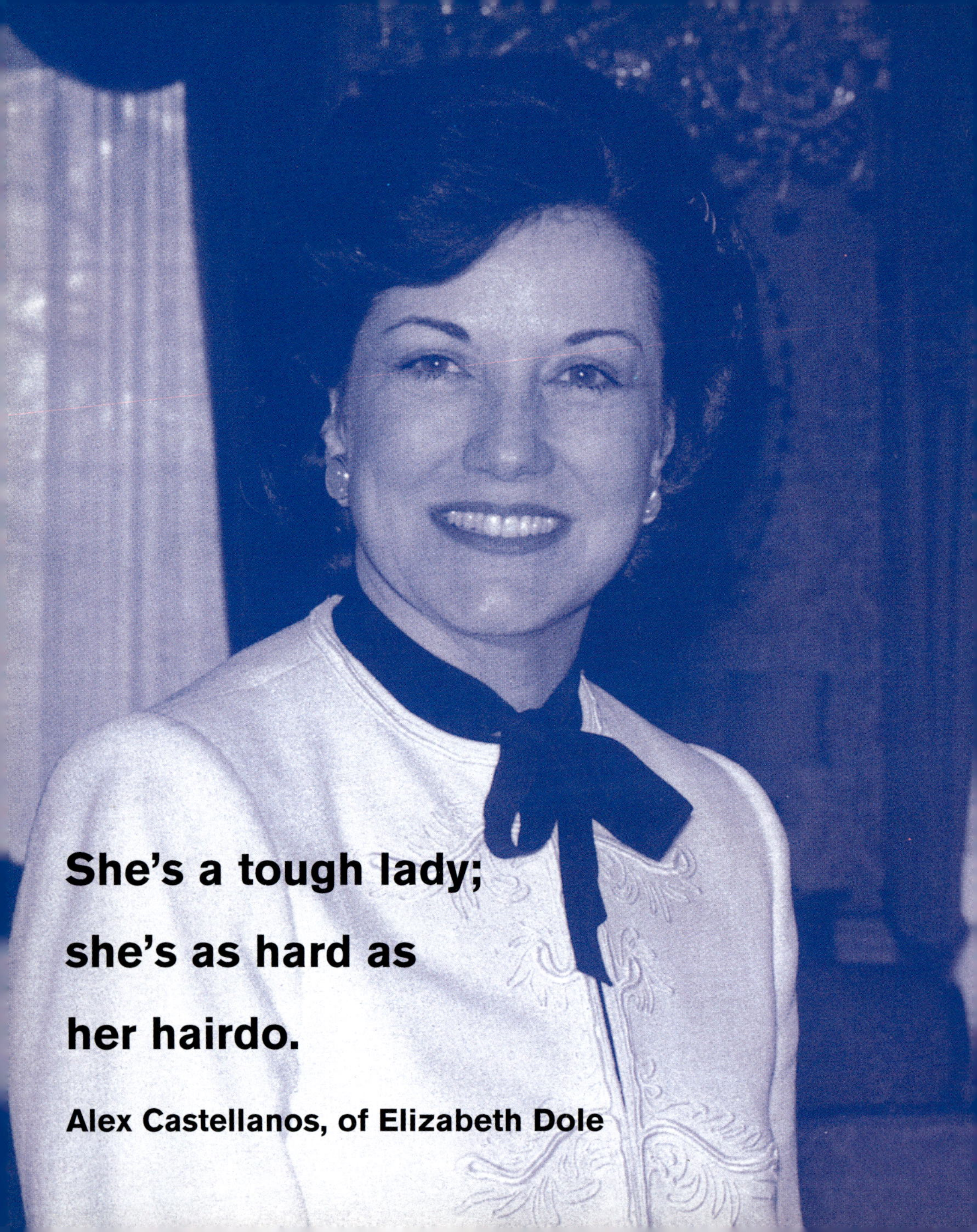

**She's a tough lady; she's as hard as her hairdo.**

**Alex Castellanos, of Elizabeth Dole**

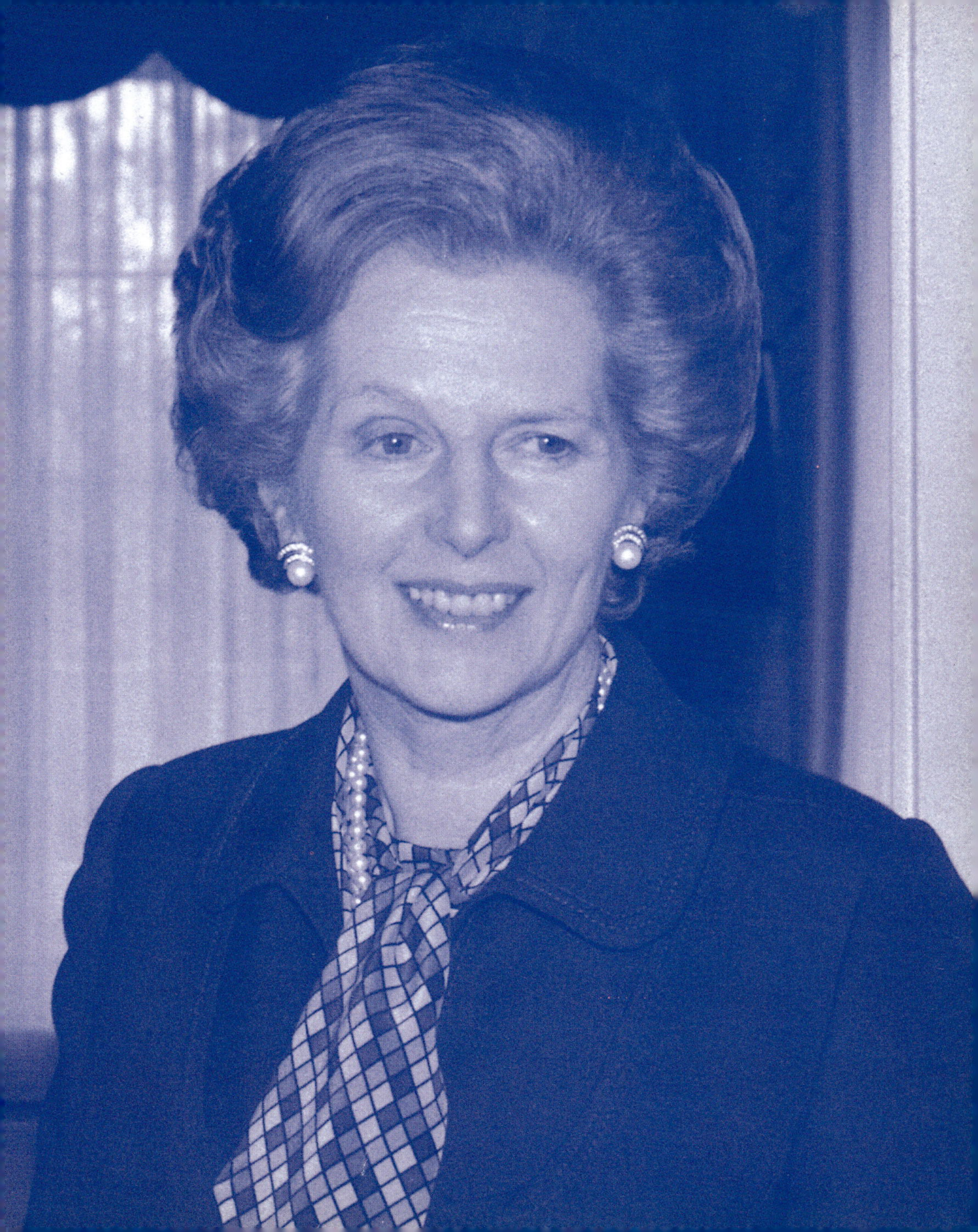

A fine head of hair adds beauty to a good face, and terror to an ugly one.

Lycurgus

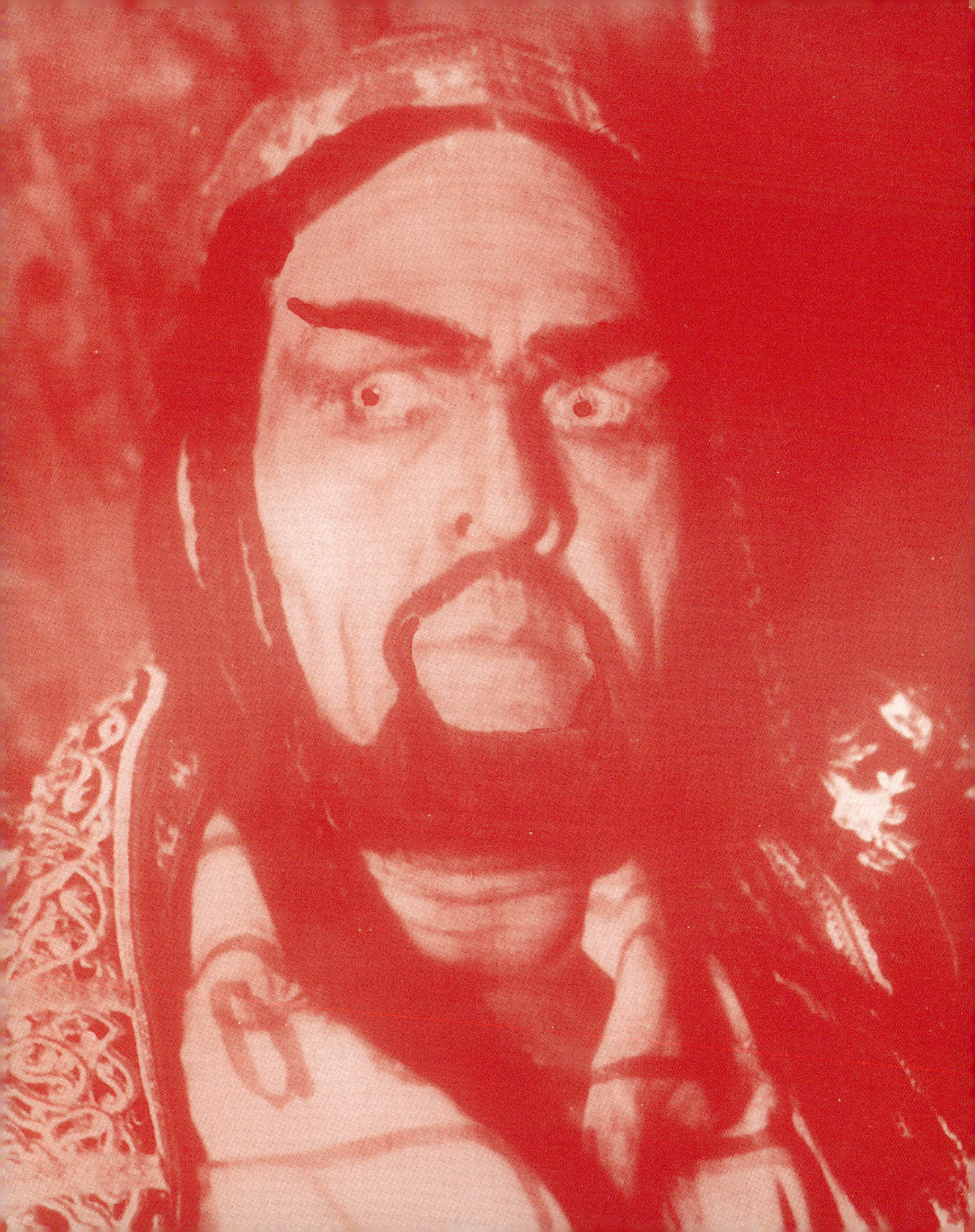

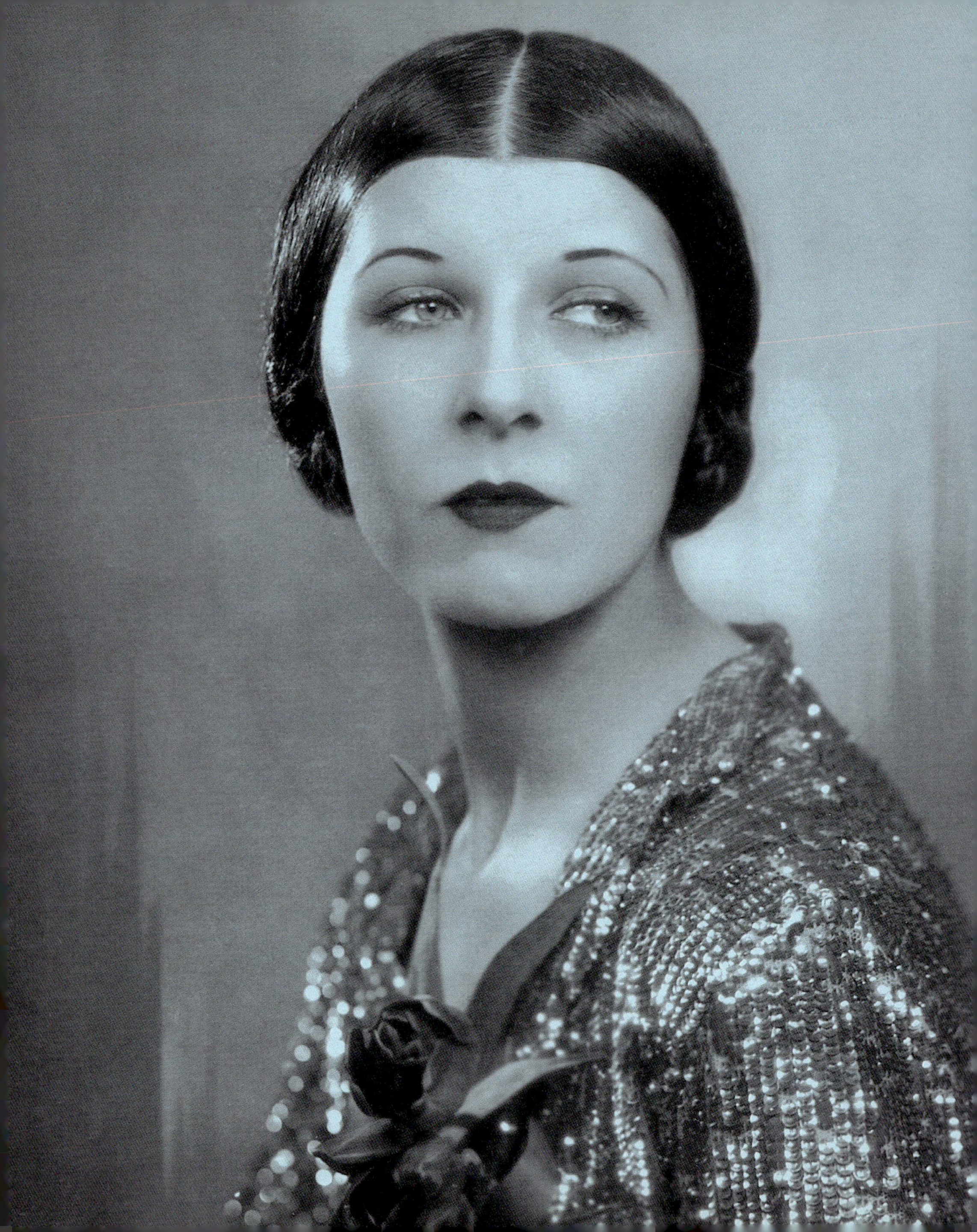

We flatten our hair on
purpose to make it
sleek and silky and to
show the shape of our
skulls, and it is our
supreme object to have
a head looking
like a wet football
on a neck as thin as
a governess' hatpin.

Cecil Beaton

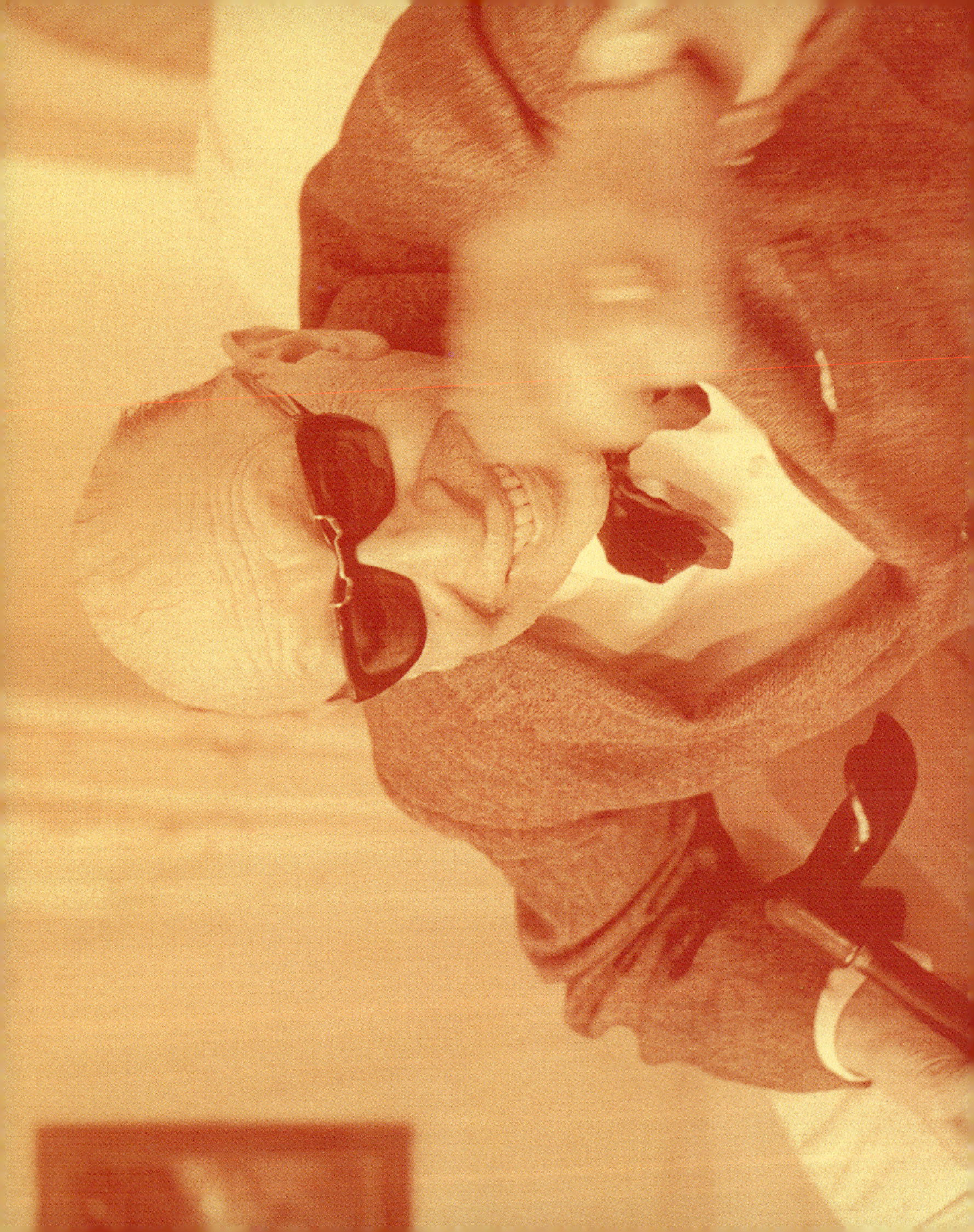

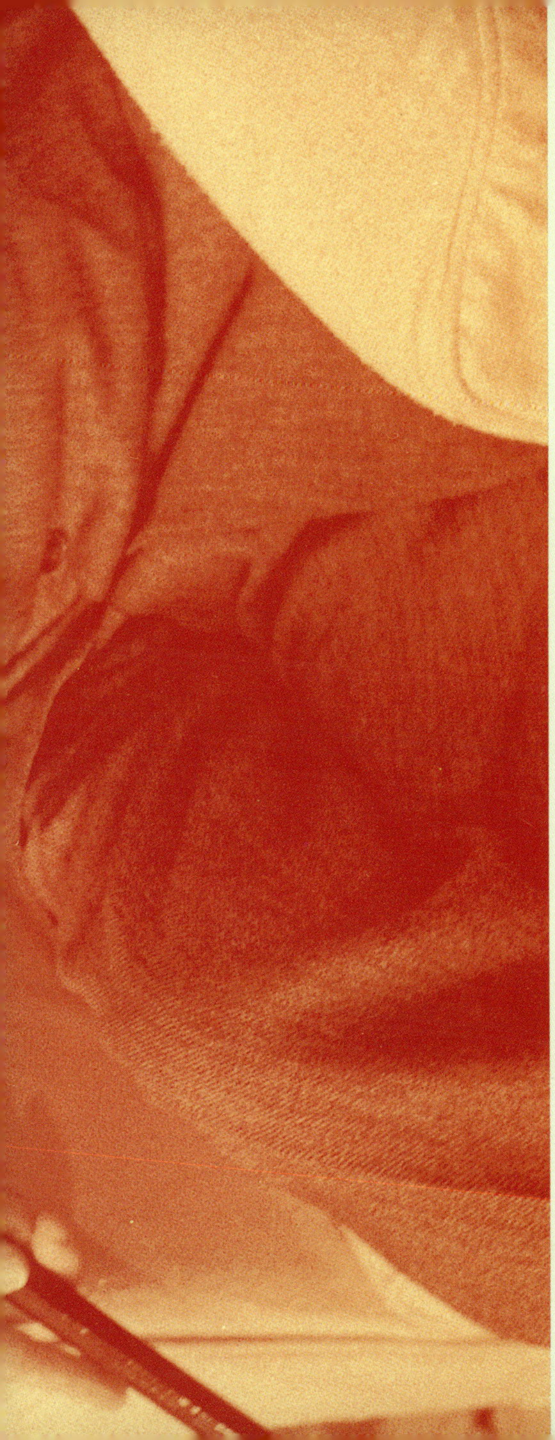

**There is more felicity on the far side of baldness than young men can possibly imagine.**

**Logan Pearsall Smith**

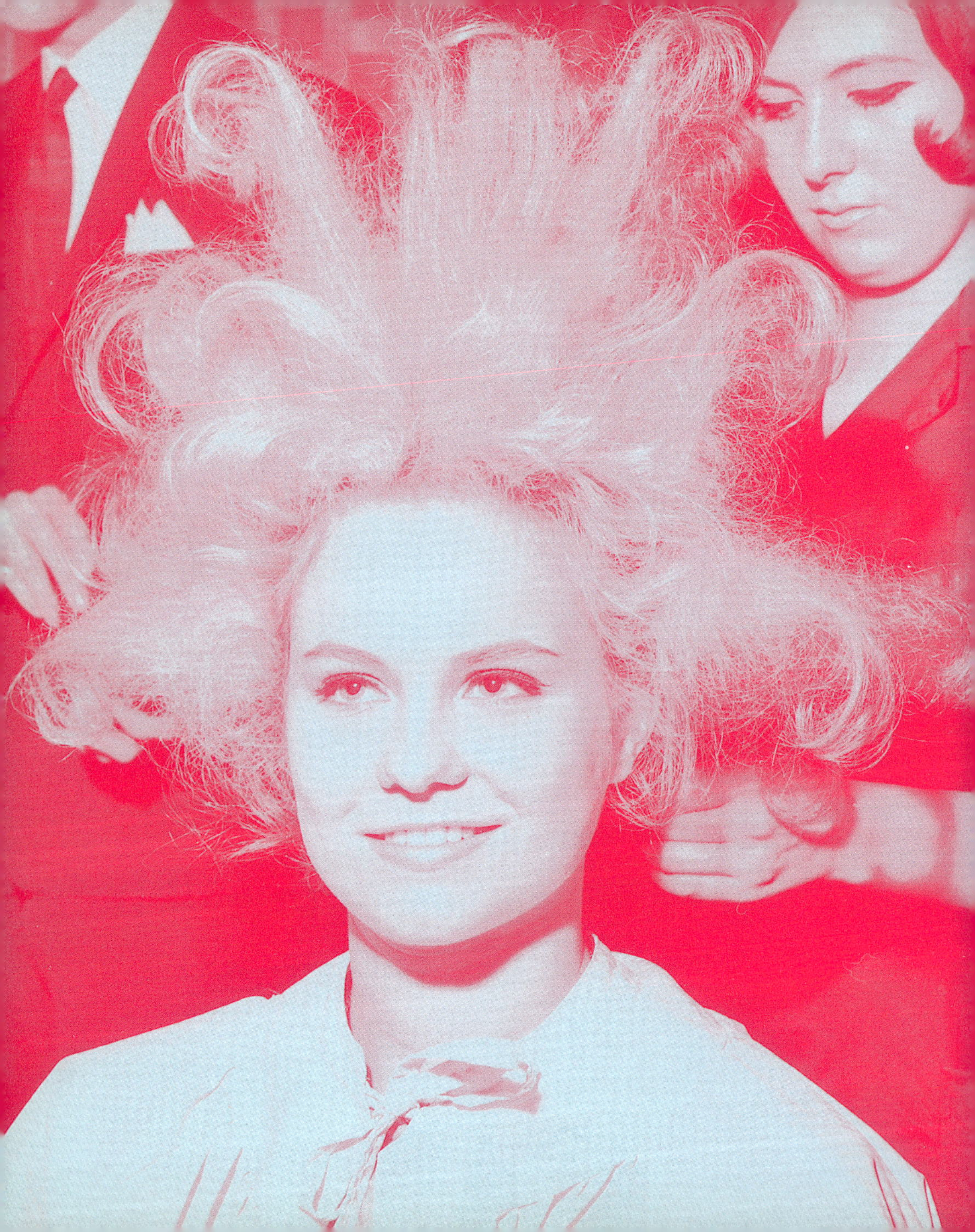

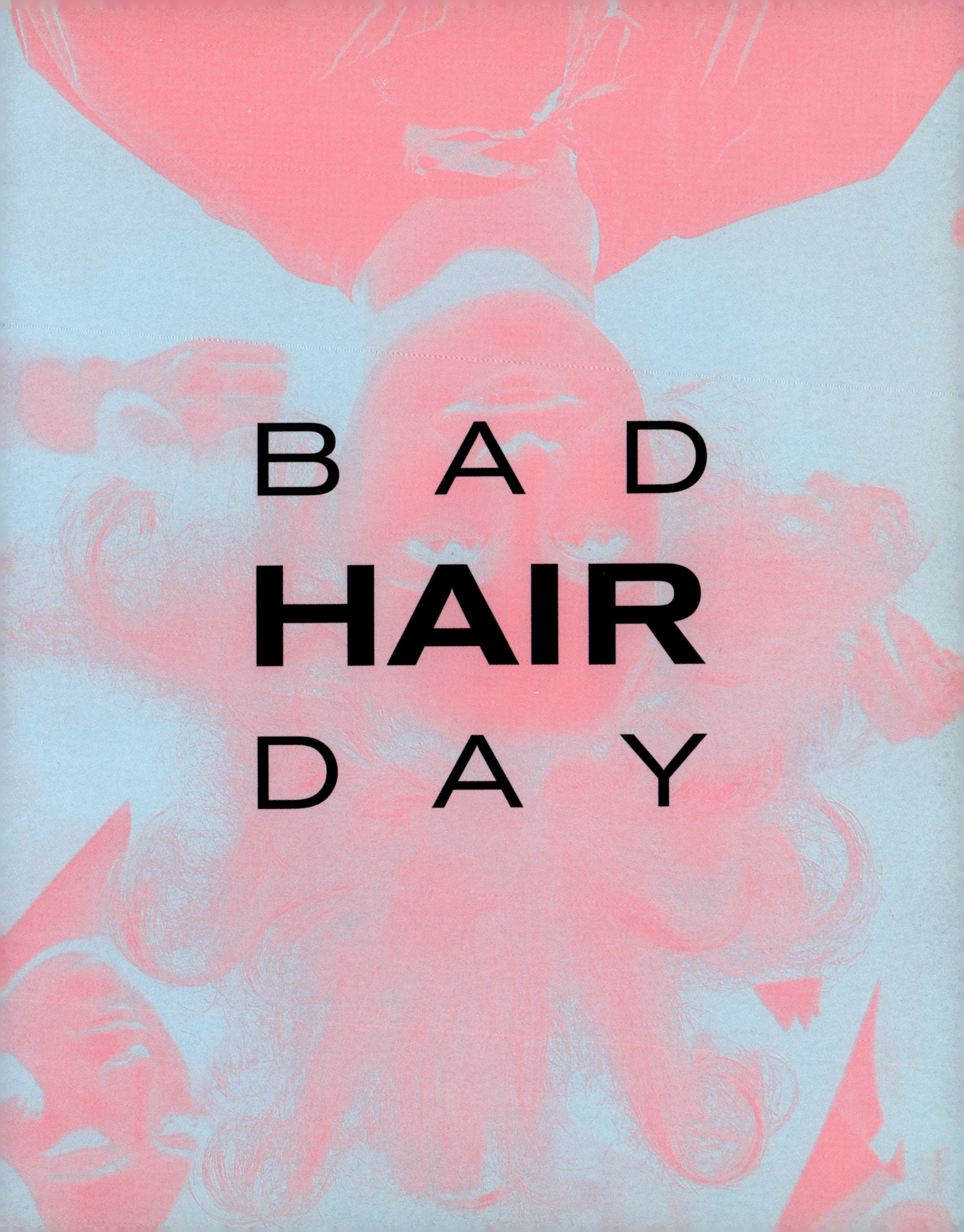

# BAD HAIR DAY

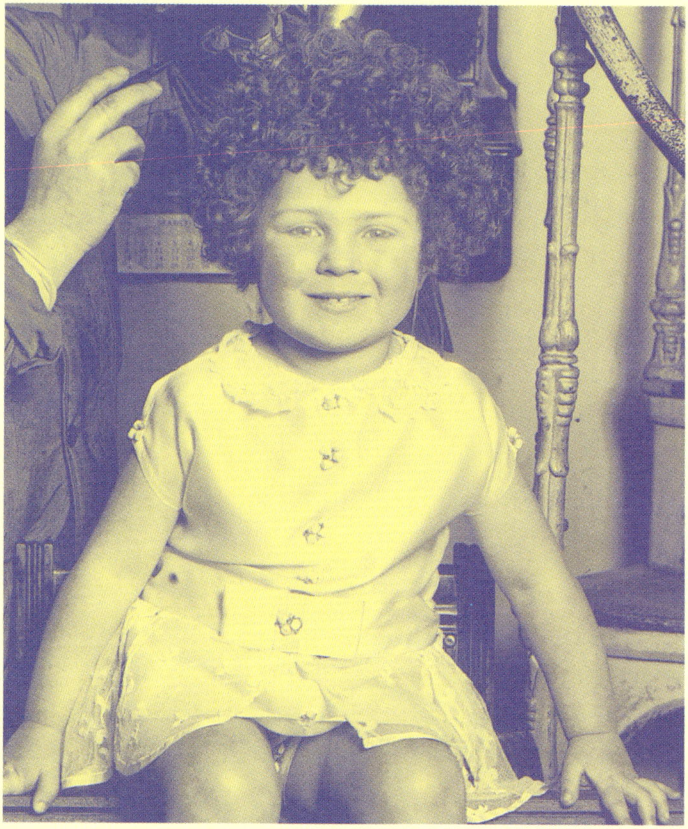

There was a little girl,
Who had a little curl,
Right in the middle of her
forehead.

And when she was good,
She was very, very good,
And when she was bad,
she was horrid.

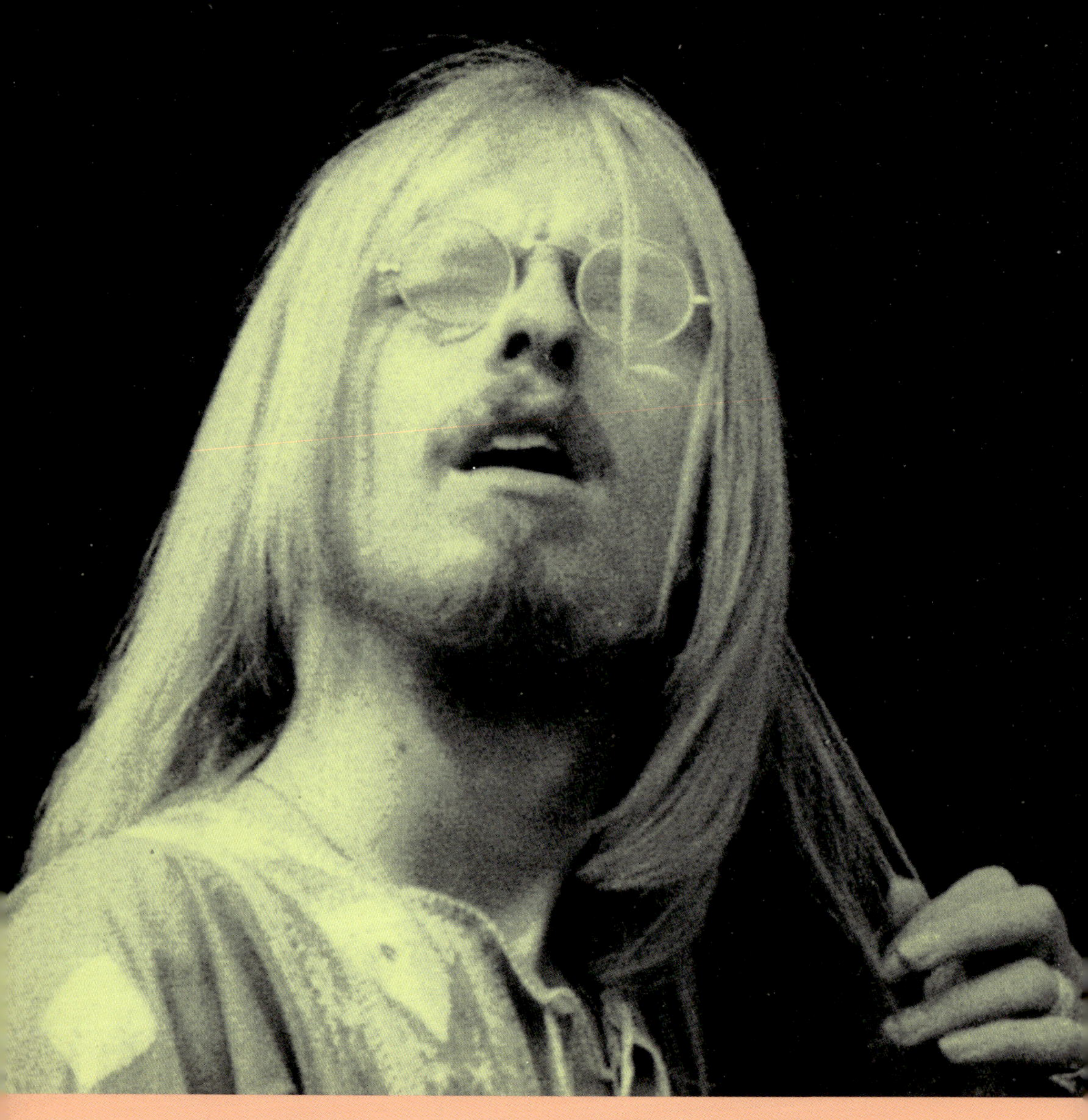

# LOVE

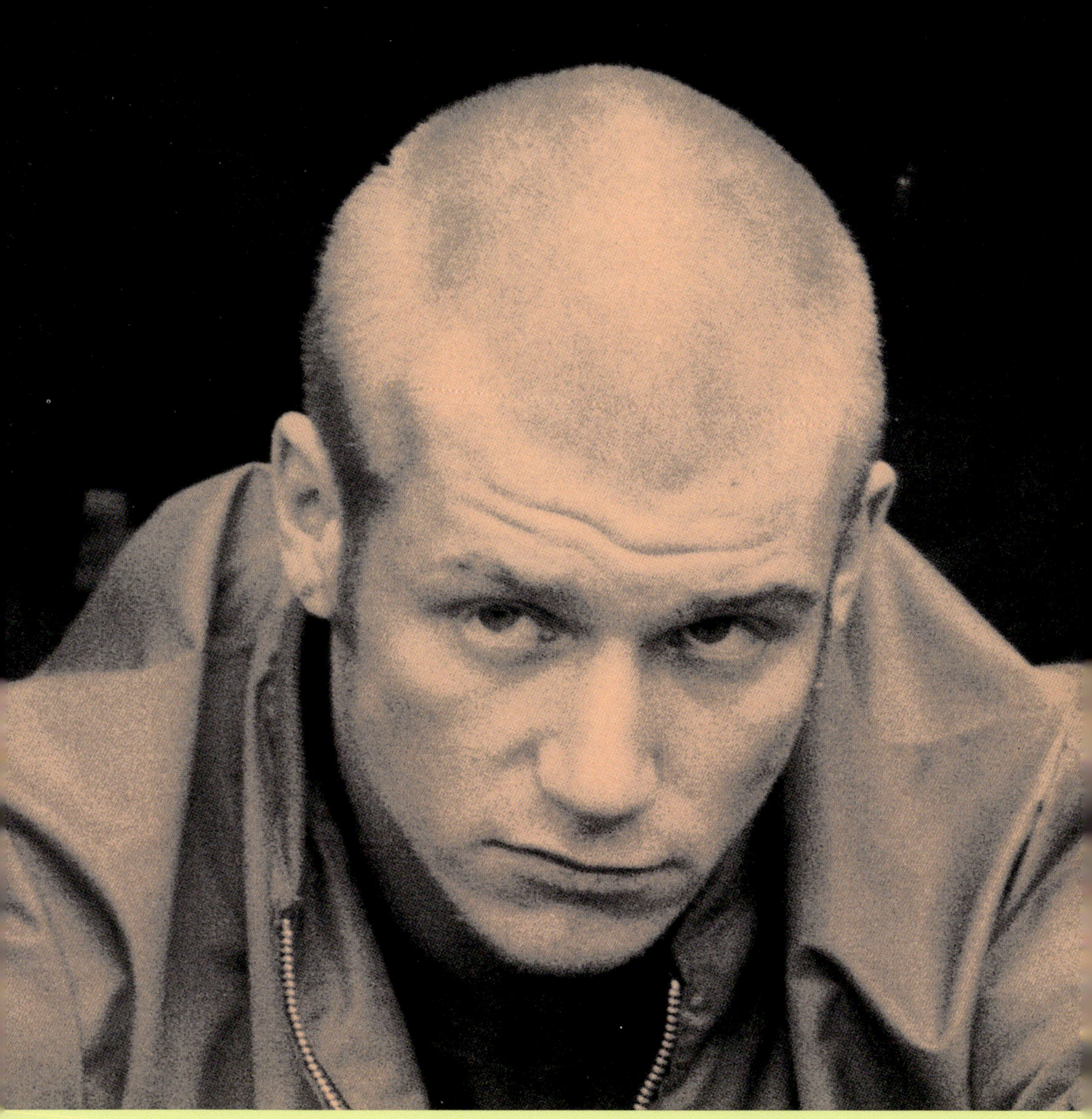

# HATE

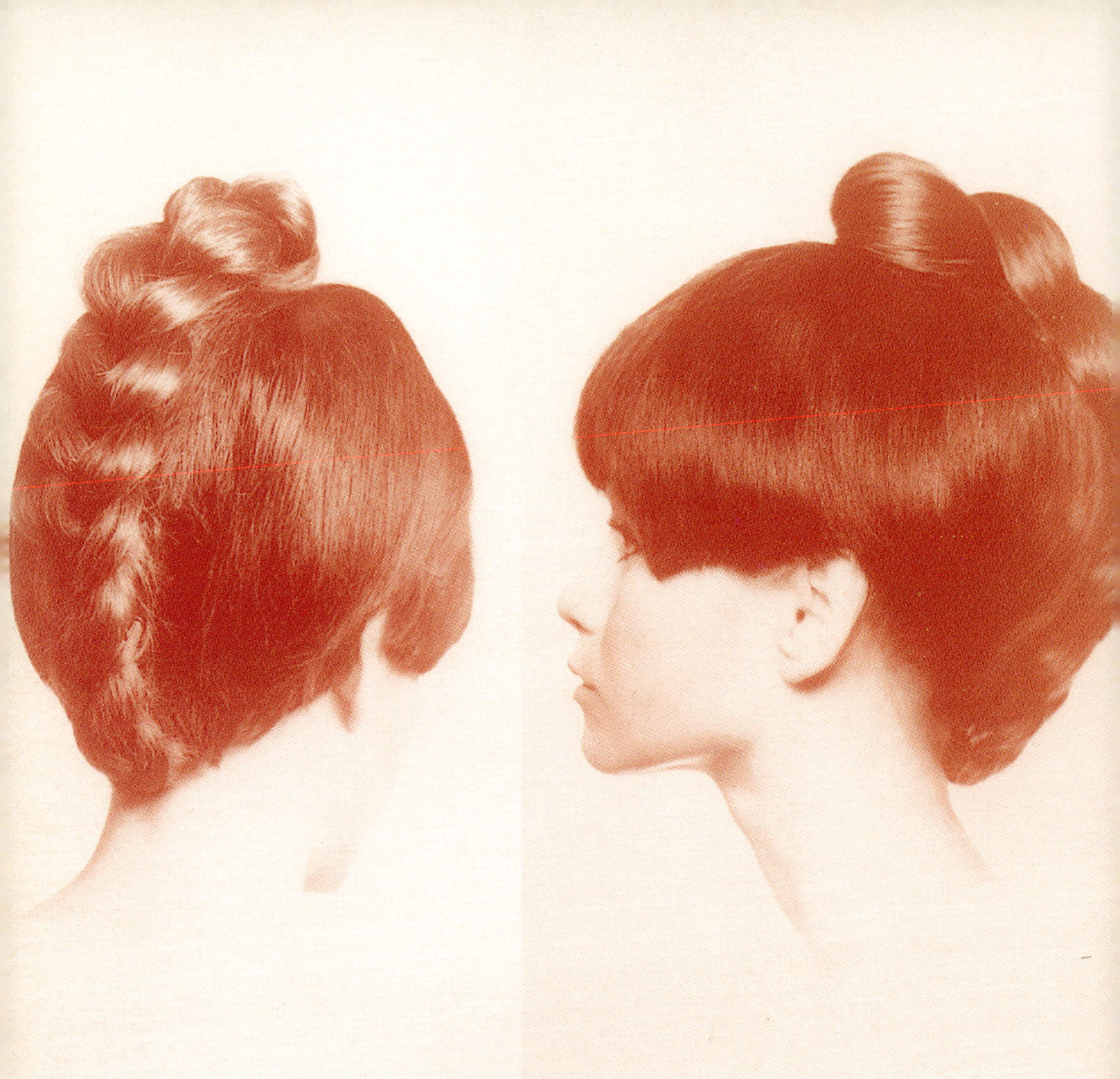

# La Centurionne

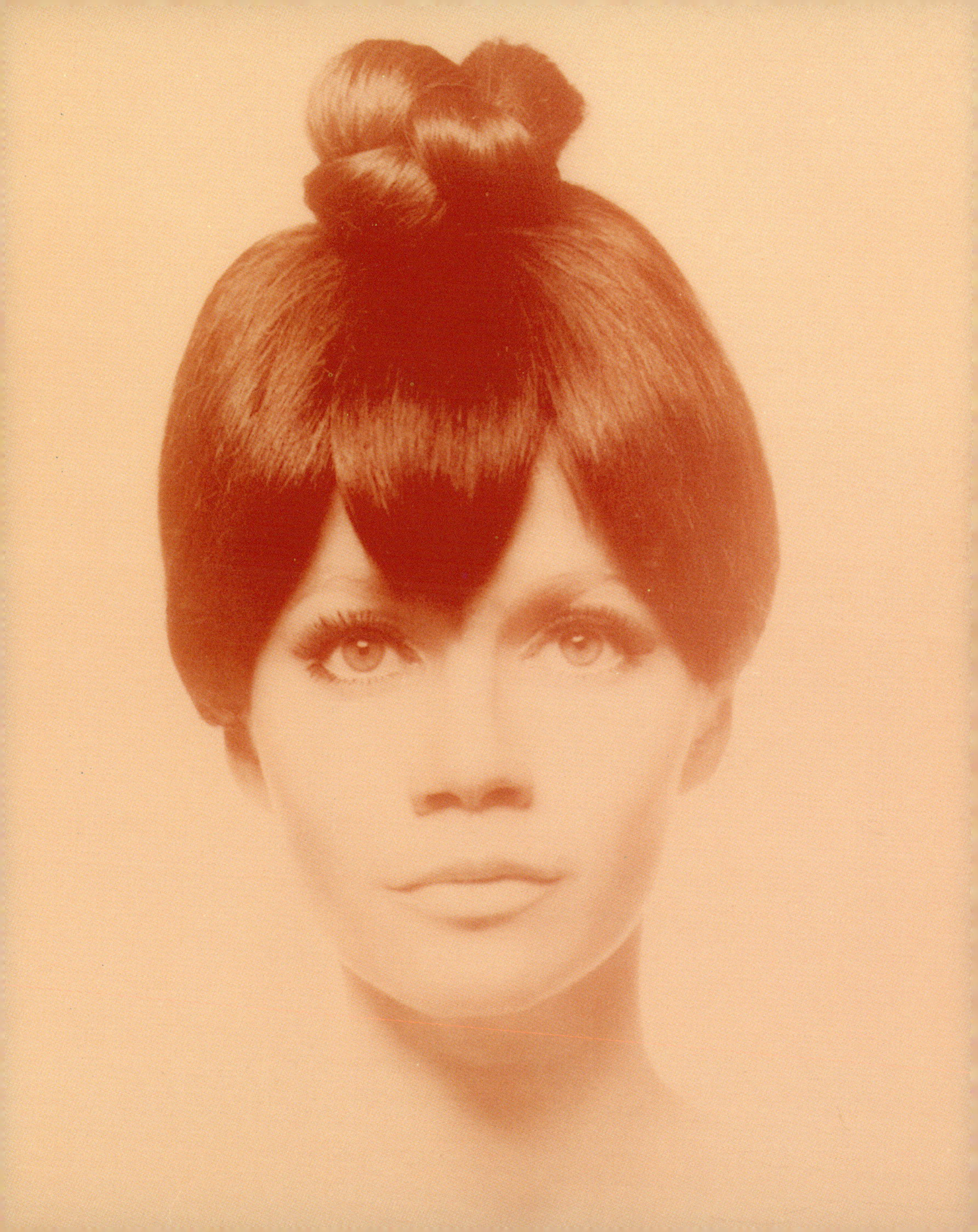

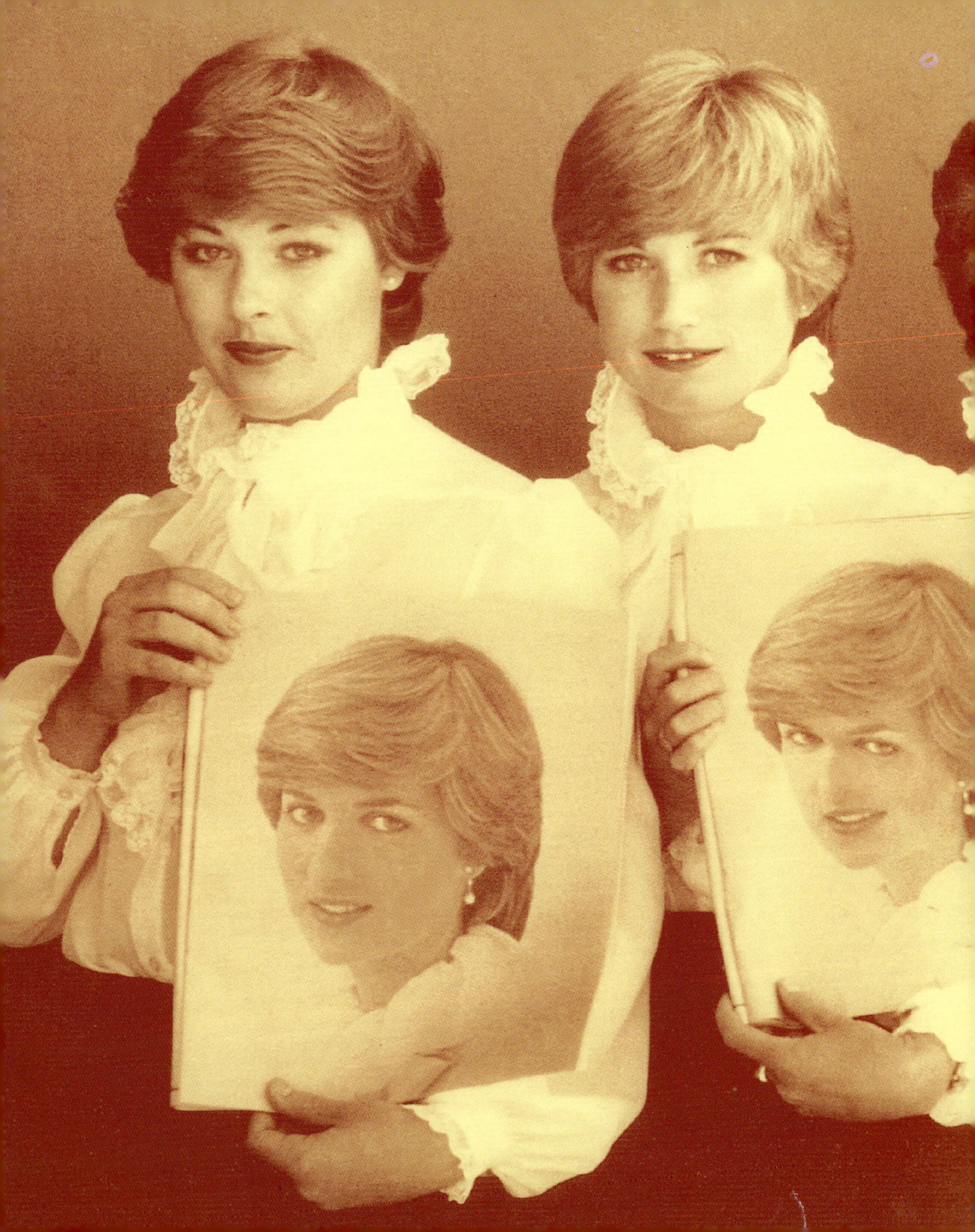

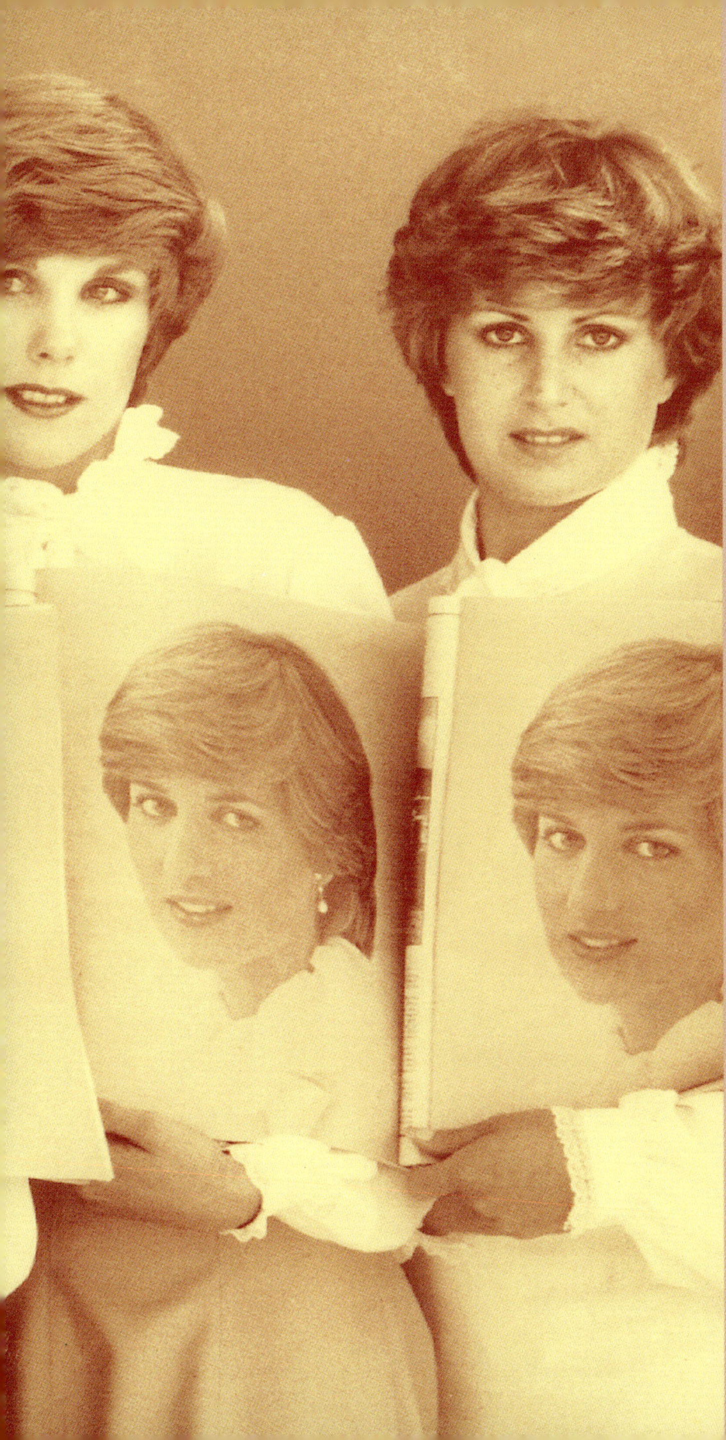

# HAIR LINE

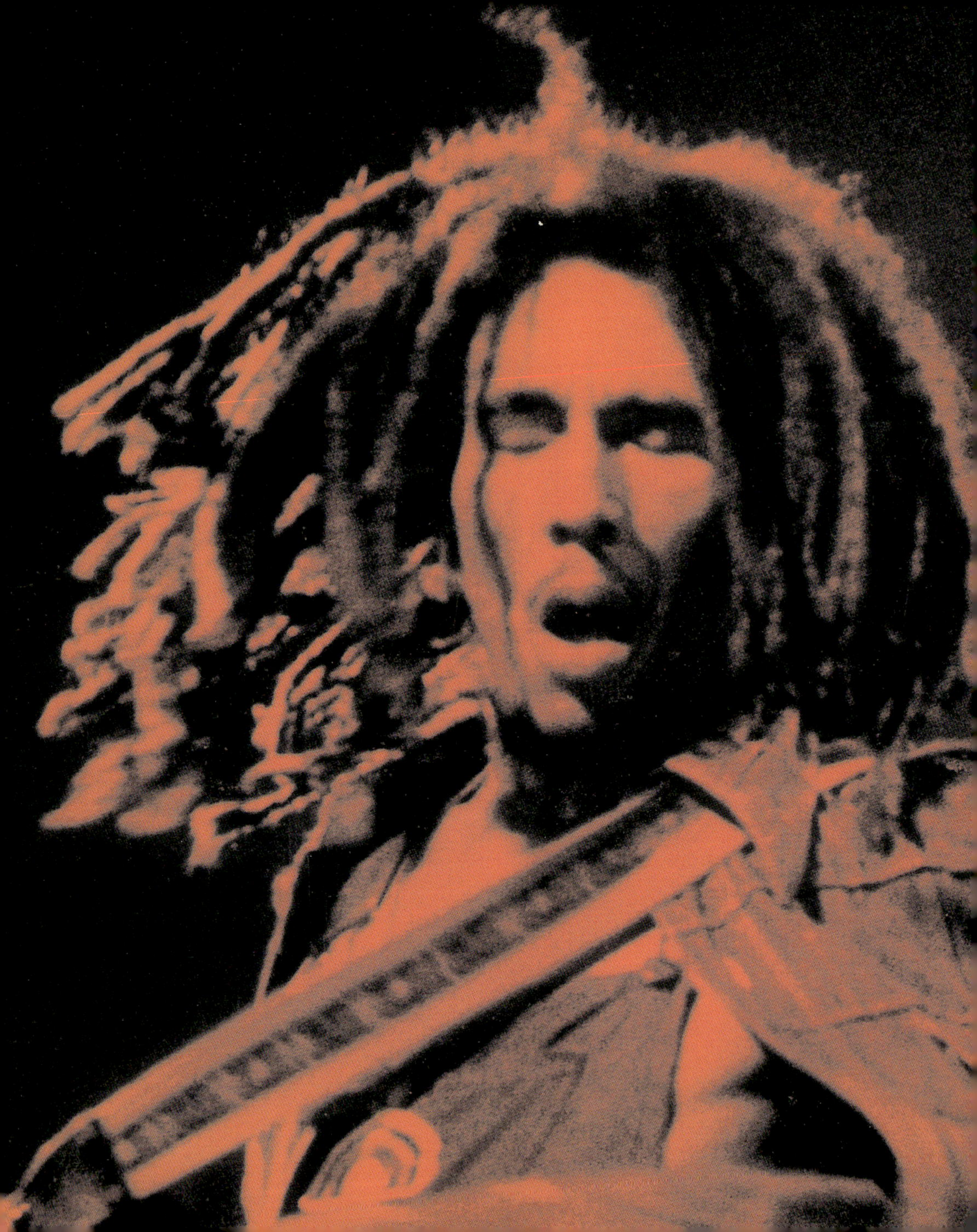

ICON

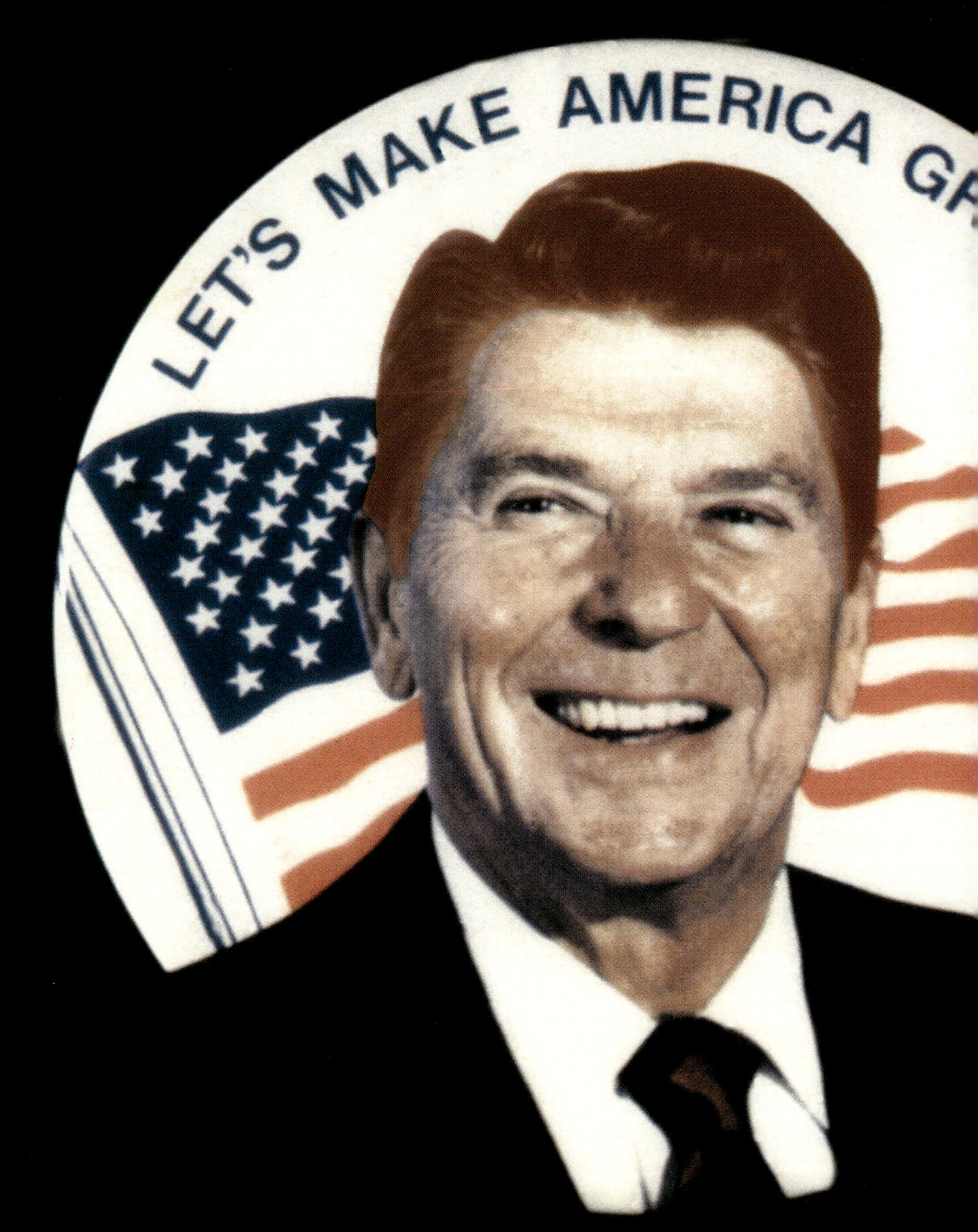
LET'S MAKE AMERICA GR

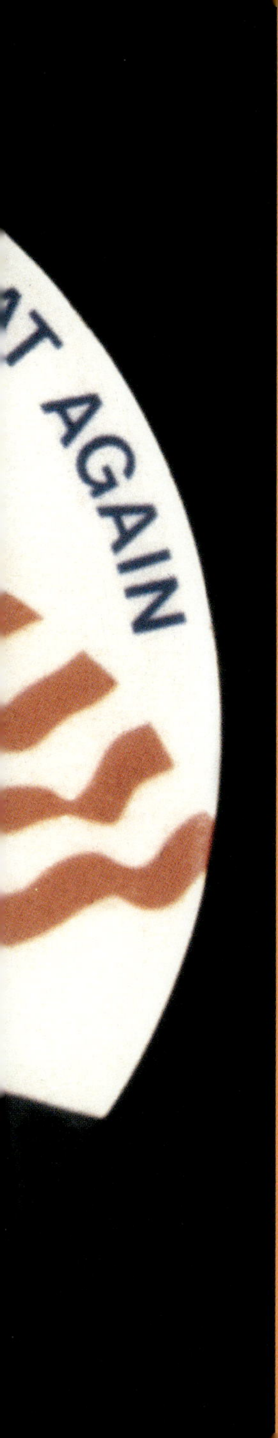


**Ronald Reagan doesn't dye his hair, he's just prematurely orange.**

**Gerald Ford**

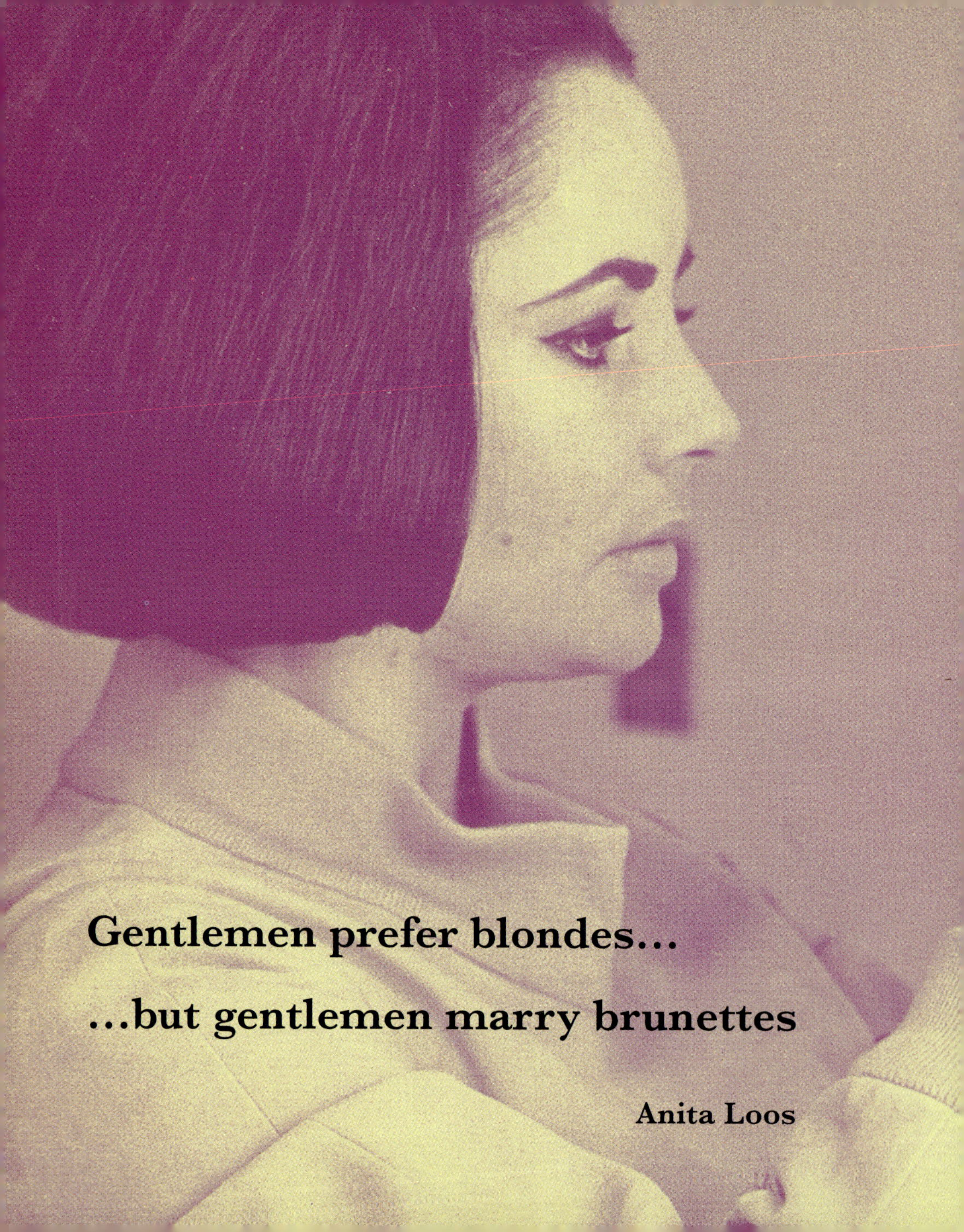
Gentlemen prefer blondes…
…but gentlemen marry brunettes
Anita Loos

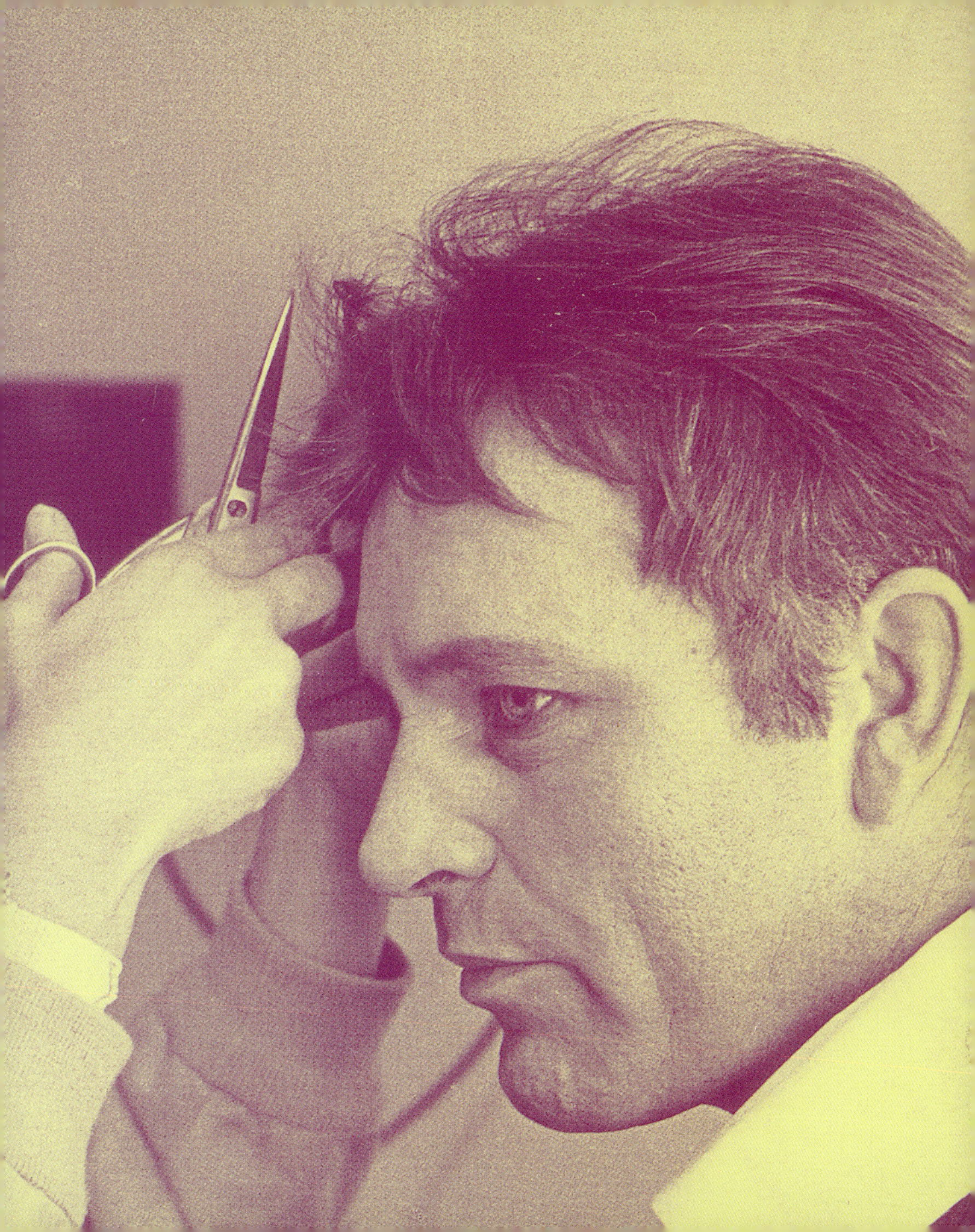

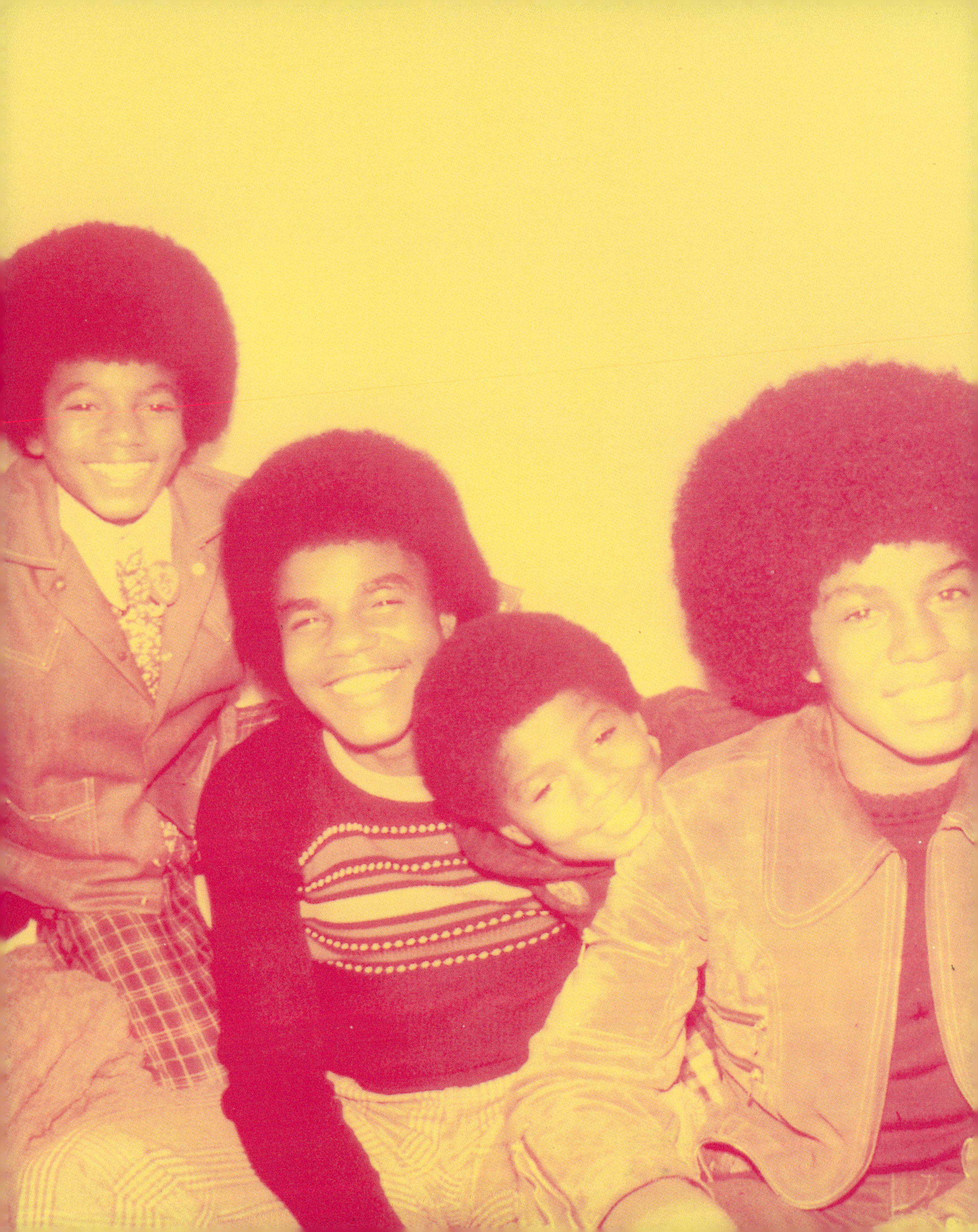

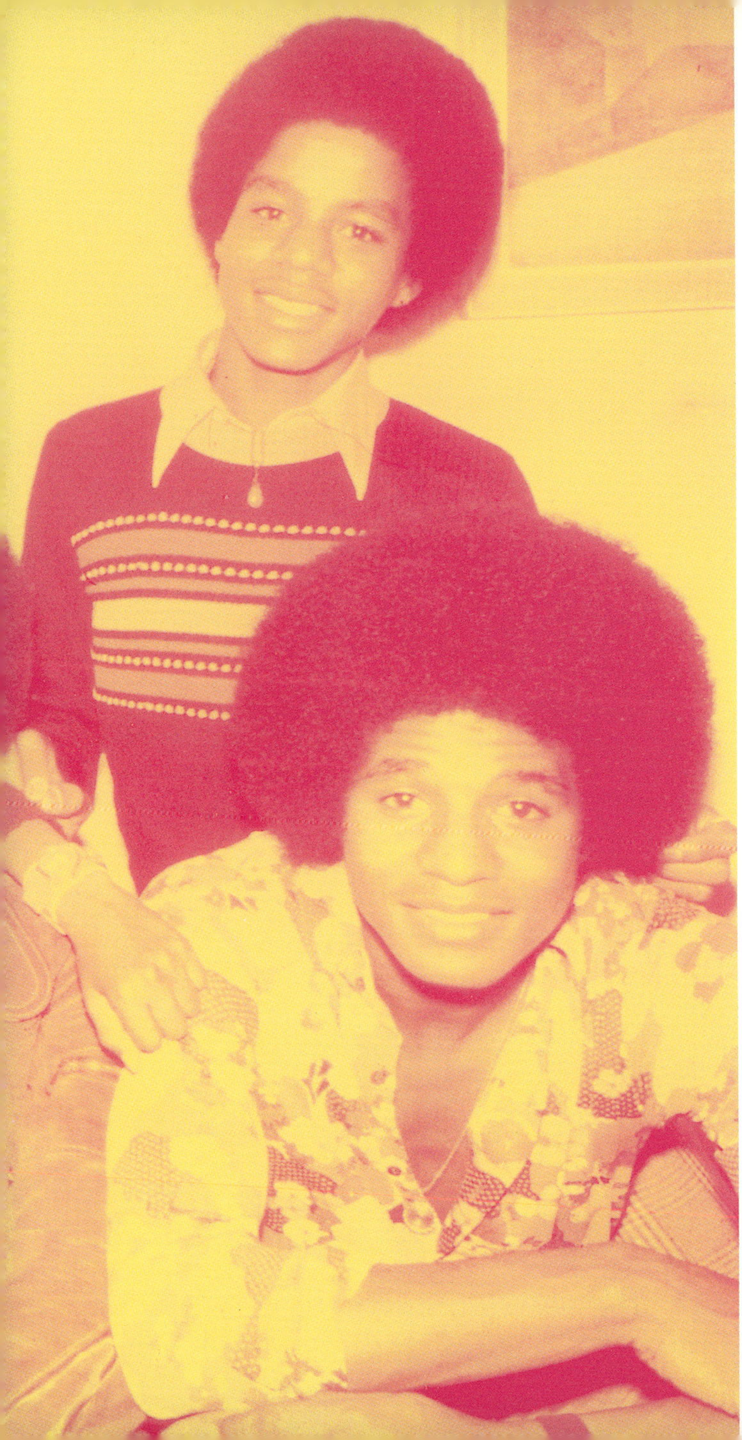

# HAIR BAND

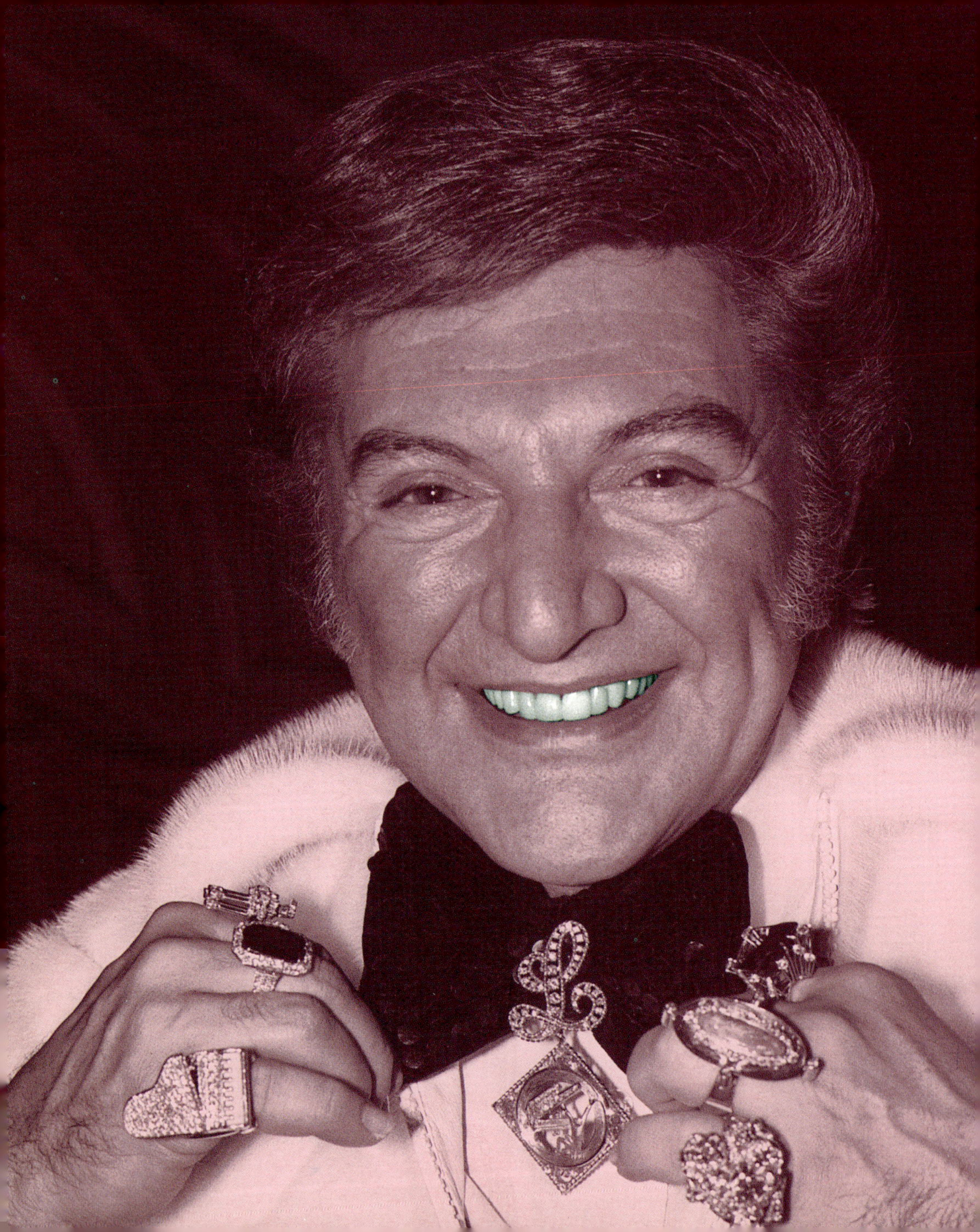

**A celebrity is any well-known T.V. or movie star who looks like he spends more than two hours working on his hair.**

**Steve Martin**

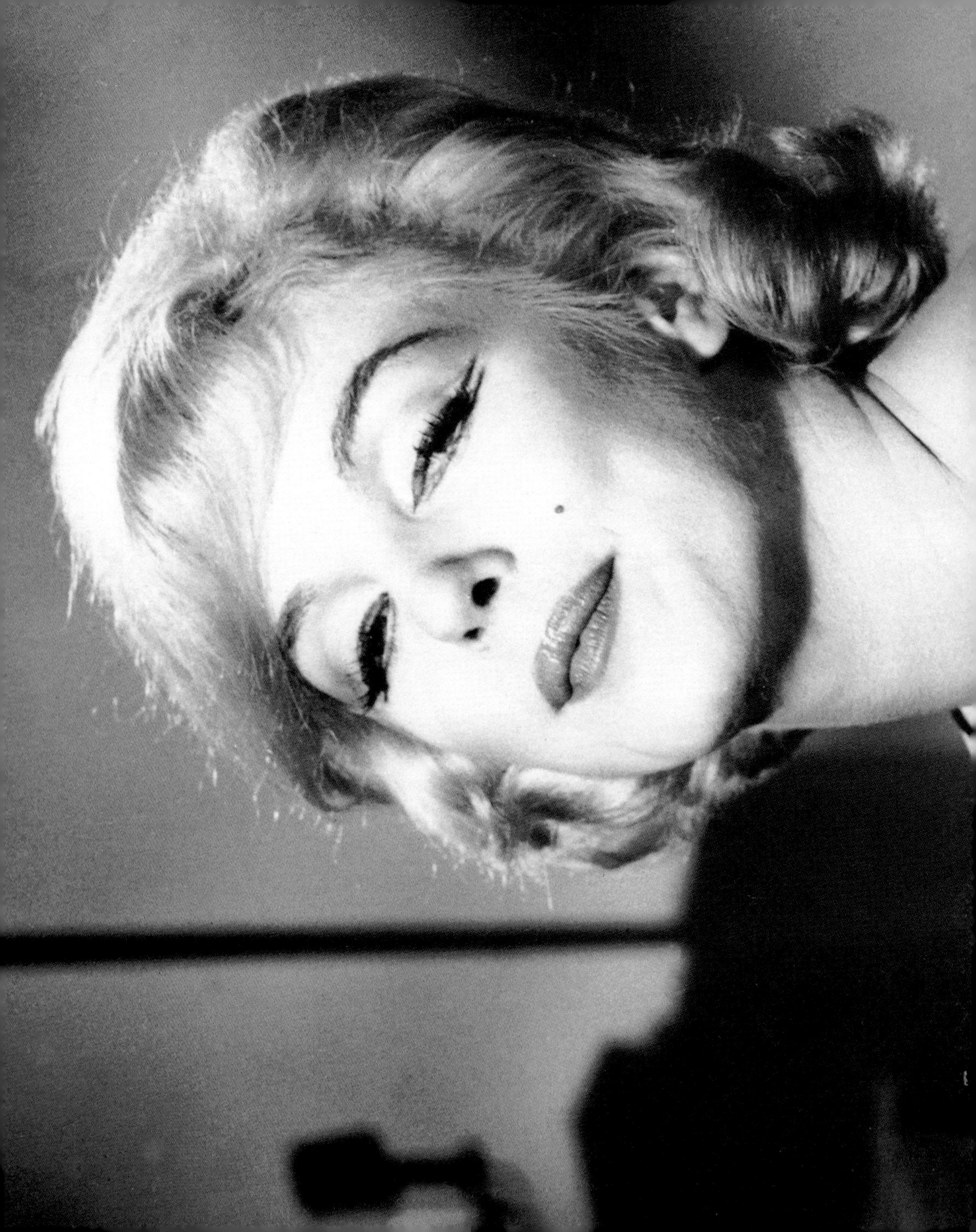

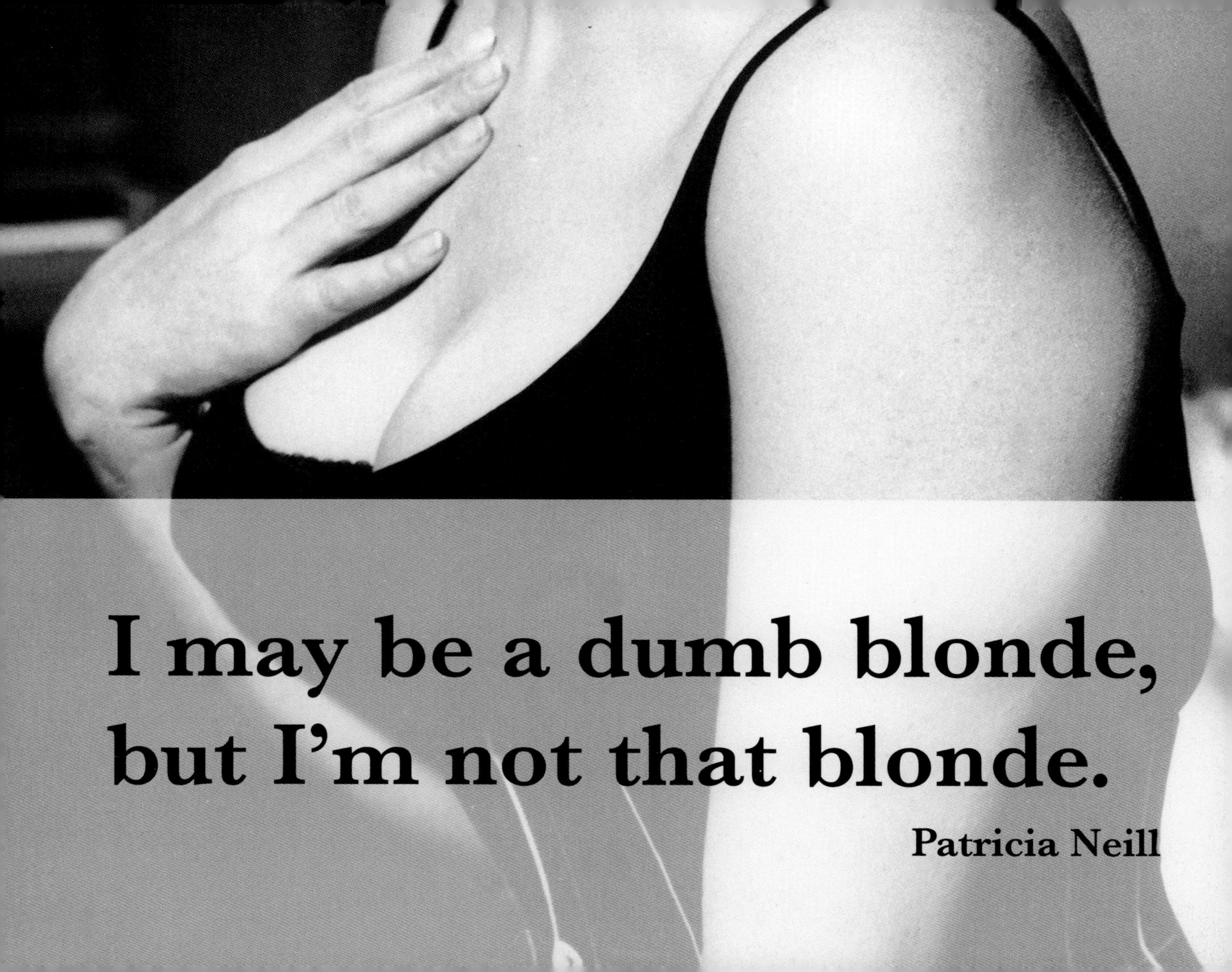

**I may be a dumb blonde,
but I'm not that blonde.**

**Patricia Neill**

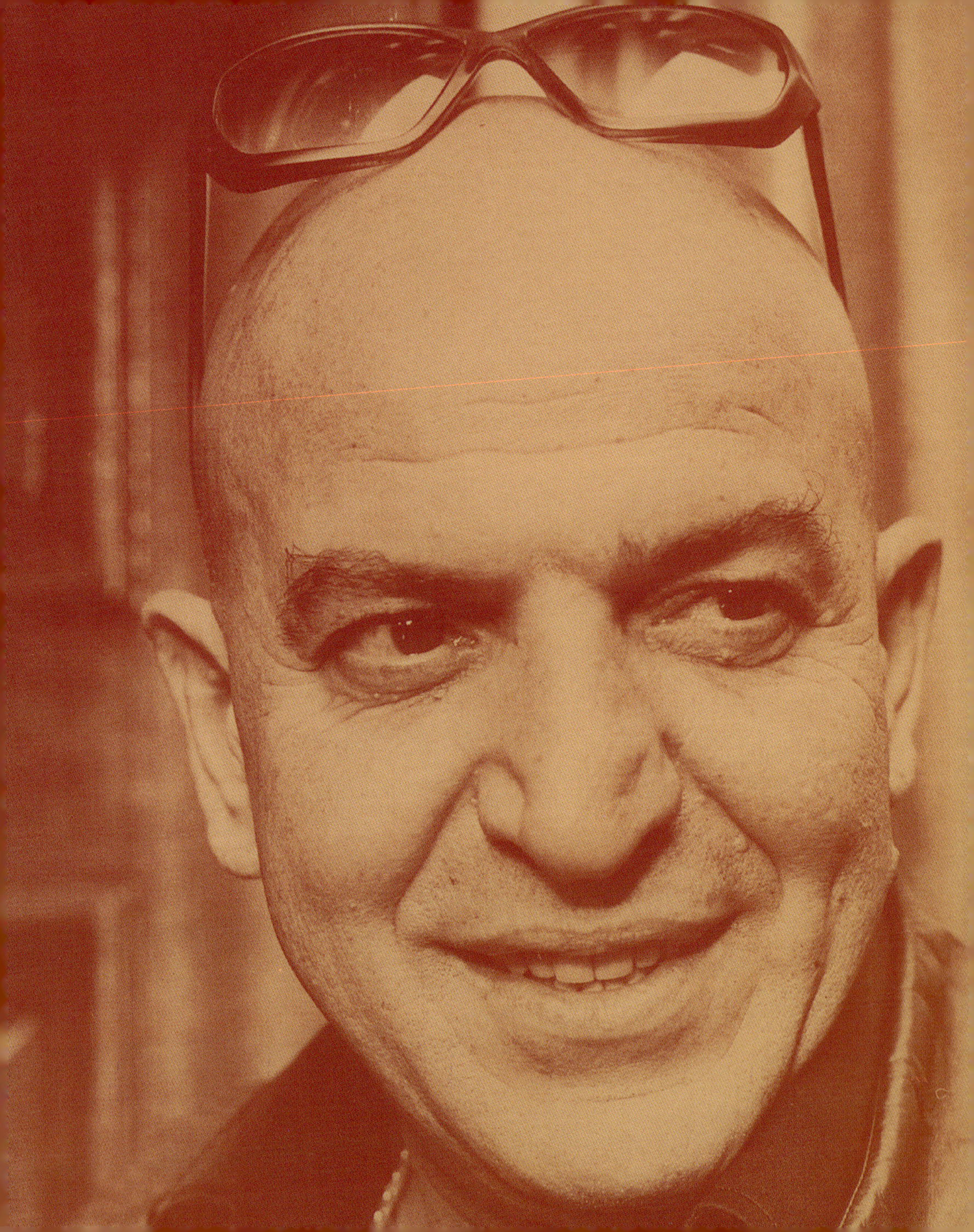

# EGG-SHELL BLONDE

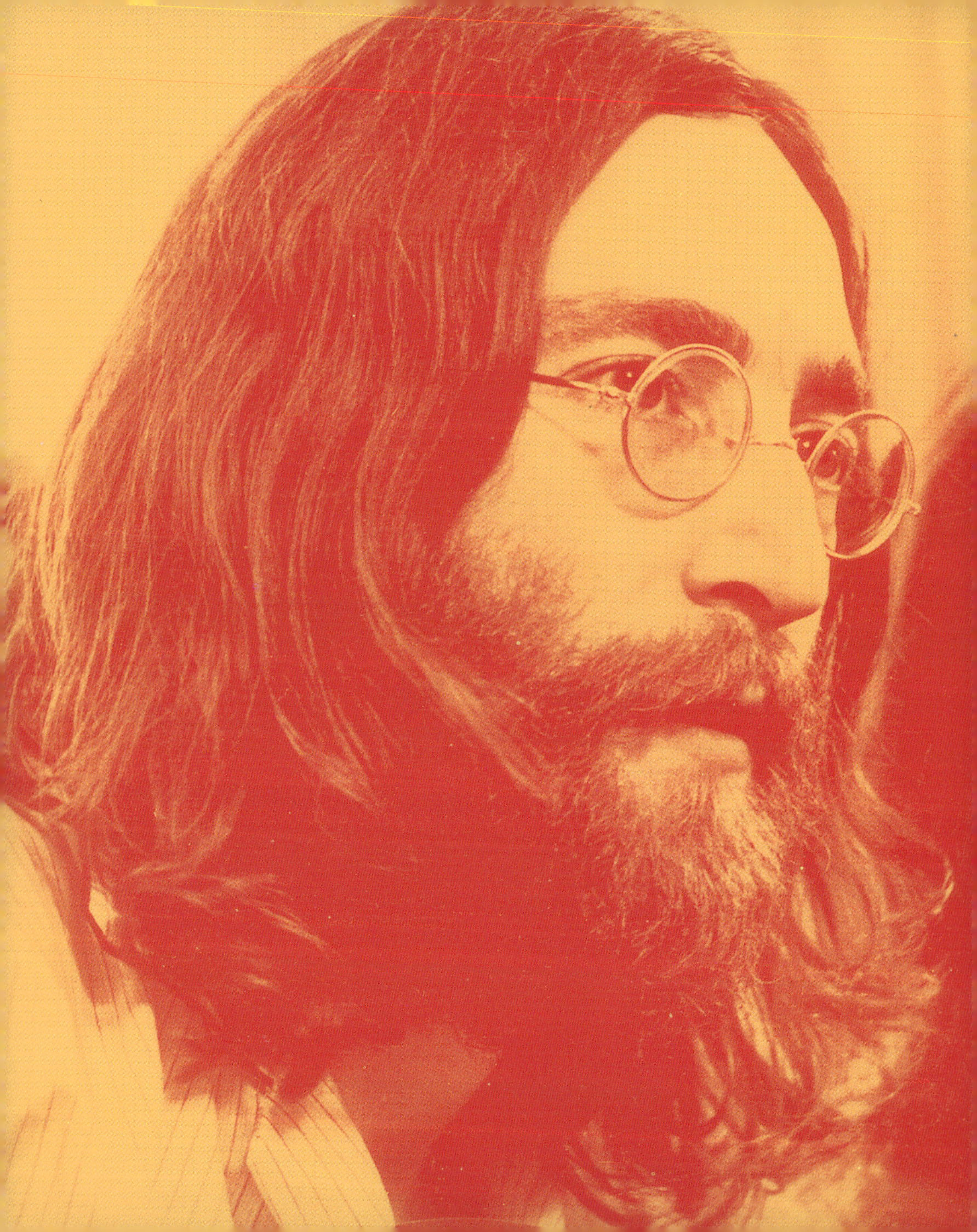

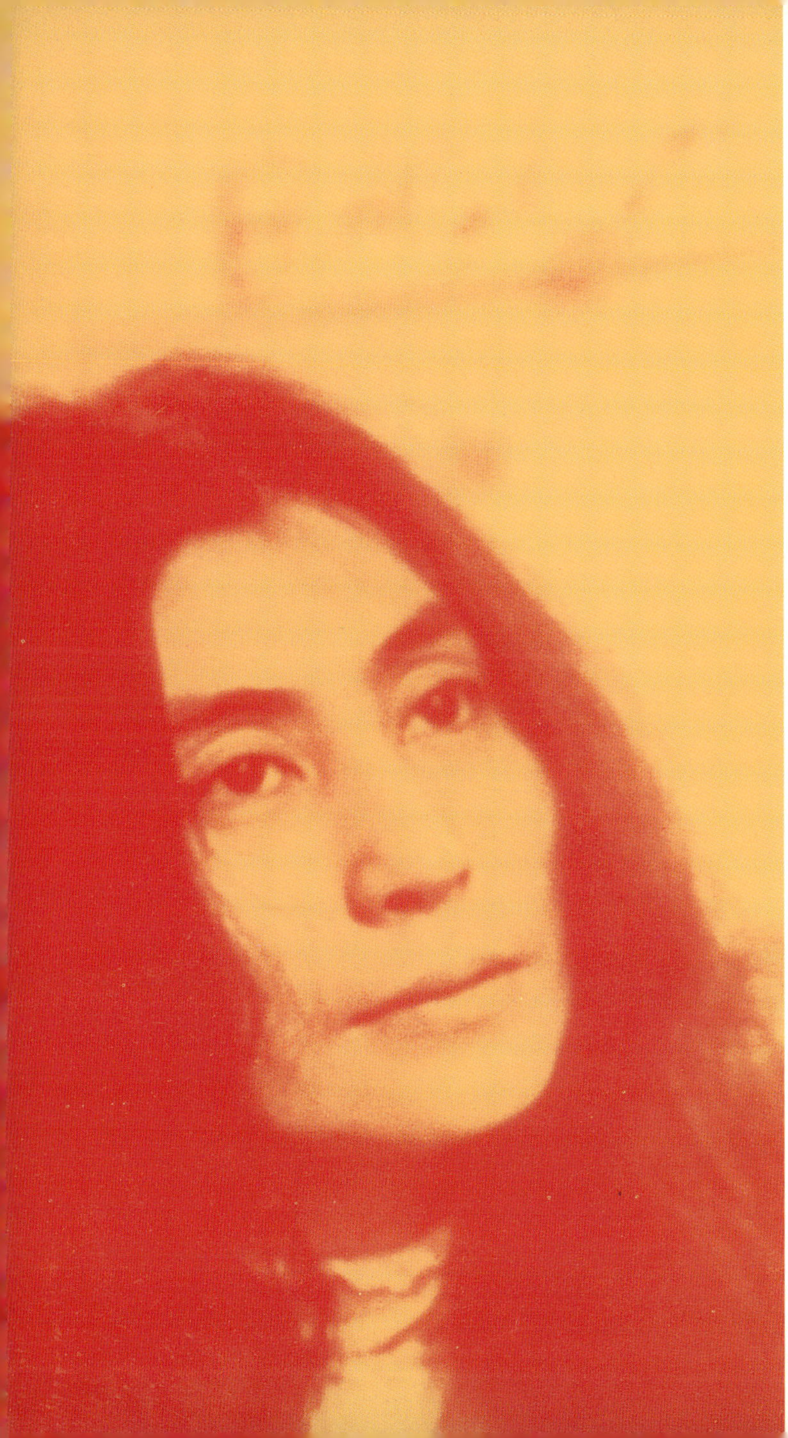

# HAIR PEACE

## Picture credits

**All images Hulton Getty Picture Collection.**

**cover, title page and page 4/5:** Jean Shrimpton modelling the 'sun' hairstyle designed by Parisian hairstylist Carita, 1965.

**page 6:** Veronica Lake in a scene from the film 'I Wanted Wings', 1941.

**page 8/9:** Three women who feature in the play 'On With The Dance' at the London Pavilion, circa 1921.

**page 10:** From top to bottom, Danish actor Jean Hersholt, 1934, Vidal Sassoon, with his wife Beverly, 1972; Cricketer Bishen Bedi, 1977.

**page 11:** Father Christmas, 1960.

**page 12:** Nancy Carroll in a scene from the film 'Devil's Holiday', 1930.

**page 14/15:** Miss Canada, a 'Miss World' contestant, 1973.

**page 16/17:** Farmers at the Sussex sheep fair, 1936.

**page 18/19:** 'Gibson Girls', Miss Carlyle and Miss Clarke take tea, circa 1905.

**page 20:** Marsha Hunt, 1968.

**page 22:** Beryl Hardesty modelling a lacquered hairstyle, 1950.

**page 23:** From top to bottom, 'The Helmet' hairstyle, 1945; 'The Beehive' hairstyle, 1938; Hairstyle, 1949.

**page 25:** Man being fitted with a wig at Alexe's Queen Street salon, 1967.

**page 26/27:** 'The Spanish Cheekbone Curl' hairstyle, 1953.

**page 28:** Electric perming machine, 1935.

**page 30/31:** American actress Frances Day, 1949.

**page 32/33:** Mary Quant having her hair cut by Vidal Sassoon, 1964.

**page 35:** Heather Goldman having her hair styled by Robert Bowman, 1969.

**page 36/37:** American singer Rita Coolidge in Hyde Park, London, 1971.

**page 38/39:** Spanish surrealist artist Salvador Dali, 1951.

**page 40/41:** The Beatles, 1964.

**page 43:** Little boy having his hair trimmed with an electric shaver, 1955.

**page 44/45:** Elizabeth Dole (left) and Margaret Thatcher (right), 1984.

**page 47:** Russian bass singer Feodor Ivanovich Chaliapin as Prince Igor, circa 1890.

**page 48:** Nancy Beard, 1929.

**page 50/51:** Russian-born composer, conductor, pianist and writer Igor Fyodorovich Stravinsky, 1965.

**page 52/53:** Miss Finland, a 'Miss World' contestant, 1964.

**page 54:** Peggy Vaff modelling a 'bubble perm', 1930.

**page 56:** Hippy at the Isle of Wight pop festival, 1970.

**page 57:** Skinhead, Notting Hill, London, 1980.

**page 58/59:** 'La Centurionne', the French winter hairstyle of 1965.

**page 60/61:** Princess Diana lookalikes in New Zealand, 1984.

**page 62/63:** Bob Marley, 1975.

**page 64/65:** Ronald Reagan, 1980.

**page 66/67:** Elizabeth Taylor giving her future husband Richard Burton a haircut.

**page 68/69:** The Jackson Five, 1972.

**page 70:** Liberace, 1980.

**page 72/73:** Marilyn Monroe in a scene from the film 'Let's Make Love', 1960.

**page 74:** Telly Savalas, 1975.

**page 76/77:** John Lennon and Yoko Ono, 1969.

Published by MQ Publications Limited
254–258 Goswell Road, London EC1V 7RL



ISBN: 1-84072-129-4

1 3 5 7 9 0 8 6 4 2



Design: John Casey
Series Editor: Elizabeth Carr

Printed and bound in Italy

---